MW00804607

A Reluctant Spirit:
A True Tale of God, Ghosts and a Skeptical Christian

Kathleen Berry

Copyright © 2013 Kathleen Berry

All rights reserved.

ISBN-13: 978-0-9898722-0-1

Dear Linda—
Thank you so
much for coming
to my class.
Remember — anything
is possible!

FOR KEN

All my best,

Kathleen
Berry

Sept. 2016

~Preface~

While I possess free will, I also know the universe has a way of nudging me in the direction that God wants me to take in life. I had intended to hide my true experience behind the guise of a novel, so no one would know this story was about *my* transformation. I had no desire to expose myself as someone I would've judged harshly years before. However, the more I pursued forging a piece of fiction, the more writing roadblocks appeared. Eleven months after Goldfield, I hadn't written past chapter 2. The Divine's gentle nudges grew stronger until I felt as though I were being hit by a redwood log. Finally, I recognized I was meant to share my story honestly. At that point, my memoir flowed from my mind and through my typing fingertips faster than I could've ever imagined.

I'm sharing my odd, eerie story to help others realize that the existence of positive spirits can be reconciled with Christianity. We are meant to interact with God's emissaries, the spirits of our departed dear ones, guardian angels and more.

This tale is told solely from my perspective, and is based on: my memories, my extensive notes and transcripts from the KTVN ghost hunts to Goldfield and the Cal Neva Lodge, as well as interviews I conducted with our Nevada Ghost Conference speakers. Thanks to KTVN Channel 2 in Reno, I was also able to refer to raw video footage and the resulting televised stories to further capture my series of events authentically.

Everything portrayed in this memoir is true in my estimation. I have changed the identities of those who requested they remain private (these instances are noted), and I have reordered minor events to increase readability.

I do not wish to convert you to believe as I do. It doesn't matter if you think ghosts exist or if you are a practicing Christian. Your truth does not need to be built upon the truths of others. We are all unique creations who need to discover our own individual relationship needs with the Greatest of All.

I wish you the best in your quest to better understand the spirit world and further your comfort level with the Most Supreme Being. And if I help one person on their journey, then putting myself out in the spotlight of ridicule is worth it.

Kathleen Berry
September 2013

~1~
B Movie

Just this morning, I embraced a deep peace, an understanding this evening would lead to something important in my life. That serenity fled a few miles back—squealing as it pushed itself through the cracked-open car window.

Faking fascination with the arid scenery we speed past, I stop making small talk with the two cordial strangers in the front seat of this SUV. They laugh in unison, responding to some joke told on satellite radio. I wipe my palms against my soft, brushed cotton pants, take a deep breath and watch the sagebrush hills turn to scrub. Although a passenger, I'm along for more than a ride.

I am venturing on this journey—for the most part willingly—to play a bit part in what seems like a 1950s horror flick, the kind airing late at night when reasonable people slumber in the comfort of their beds. Unfortunately, the B movie I'm to appear in isn't scripted; it's reality. For tonight, a Reno television news crew, three paranormal investigators and I (the fraidy cat) are to spend the night in reputedly one of the nation's most haunted locales: the Goldfield Hotel. I'm the designated impartial observer.

My stomach flutters. *I'm actually going to do this*? Me, the number one coward. The one who covers her eyes during the scary parts of movies. The woman who shuts the closet door tight before going to bed so she doesn't have to look into a black hole.

Nothing will happen. The building might creak. But that'll be it. After all, this isn't Hollywood. I take a deep breath.

We hurtle—at least in my angst-ridden mind—through this landscape I once drove through on my way to Vegas and points south. As we round a bend, the central Nevada town of Goldfield unveils itself. Once a city teeming with more than 20,000 souls, only a few more than 400 call it home today. Skeletal head frames dot the northern end of town, a testimony to Goldfield's once thriving mines. Clapboard houses disintegrate, long neglected. Contrails—new and blurred—crisscross the powder blue sky. And the eerie-looking Joshua trees stand like posed stick figures on the parched landscape. But it's the hotel that commands my attention. So large. So looming. Dwarfing all the structures still clinging to these desert knolls. It imposes itself on the entire community. On me.

Our small convoy—the news van with all the equipment, the ghost hunter's car and an SUV carrying me, the news anchor and executive producer—parks just south of the hotel. The SUV's engine dies and quiets. My car mates look at each other. No one speaks. Are they stunned into silence as well?

We open the doors and slide out. When we close them, the noise echoes off the buildings and down the street. Its reverberations spark action.

"Let's get some establishing shots," the anchor calls over to the photographer getting out of the news van parked beside us.

"We'll get the caretaker," Janice Oberding—my friend and the first ghost hunter I ever met—yells to us from the other car.

Everyone scatters while I stand on the thinning asphalt street, called Columbia. The news guys discuss their plan of action and set up gear. The ghost hunters sprint along a dirt road, disappearing down a small hill.

I'm alone.

My muscles throb with each movement. Every joint screams as I fight the gravity threatening to pull me into the earth itself. I'd handle tonight better if I felt stronger physically. Free of pain. I'm fighting another exacerbation of the Chronic Fatigue Syndrome (CFS) and Post-Viral Neurasthenia that's plagued me since an African photo safari almost 18 years ago.

And everything this evening entails—staying up all night in a potential adrenaline-inducing atmosphere with few places to sit or lie down—will affect me for weeks to come.

God, how did I get myself into this?

I stare at the long-vacant hotel. Slowly creep toward it. This four-story mass of brick and Nevada-quarried stone, dubbed the Gem of the Desert, had been the place to be. Once adorned in leather, mahogany and Brussels carpet, this grand lady suffered an unglamorous demise. She's been stripped bare, and there's no electricity, running water or beds.

Goldfield Hotel. Photo by Ken M. Johns

I gaze at her bank of naked windows. Fleetingly, I fancy her panes stare back at me.

Stop it!

Over by the Channel 2 Coverage You Can Count On van, voices register high, tinged with excitement.

I have as much ghost hunting experience as the average person. *None.* I don't even watch those silly paranormal shows. And I really wouldn't tune in even if I did subscribe to cable.

What brought me to the brink of this preposterous situation started four or so years ago when my employer, Truckee Meadows Community College, offered its first ghost-hunting course. As the department's public relations coordinator, I work with the media. And every fall, they take an interest in our ghost classes. I pair up journalists with paranormal investigators or psychics as they breeze through "haunted" houses and such. Never before had one of the reporters asked me to join them. Until now.

So here I am, possibly flinging myself through Hell's gate.

The air's breathless. Dry. Dusty. Only when a semi pushes through town on Highway 95 do I feel the slightest breeze against my cheek.

More voices. Laughing. I glance over to the news van and see the ghost hunters have returned with the hotel's caretaker, a petite, neatly groomed, gray-haired woman. I should go meet her. It's the polite thing to do.

Instead, I'm drawn to a first floor window—the only one not paneled with cracked plywood. My curiosity propels me to it.

The window's grimy, so I rub a small spot on the glass and cup my hands like a viewfinder. Dust shrouds everything off-white. A wall-length, carved wood bar. A sawhorse. I can't see anything else from this vantage point.

Owning this building brings on a financial curse, I've heard. No entrepreneur in the past 90-plus years made a profit. One owner even staked three mining claims—including one in the hotel basement—and still never turned a buck.

"Kathy, you ready?"

I jump, startled, and turn toward the voice. Janice resembles someone's young, perky grandmother with her dimpled cheeks, kind hazel eyes and short, curly, reddish-brown hair with a mind of its own.

I force confidence into my voice as I rub my dirty hands on my jeans. "Yes. I've always wondered what it's like inside."

She winks and lowers her voice. "It'll be all right. *You* will be all right. Okay?"

I nod.

"It's time." She pivots in the direction of the porch where the others wait.

I grasp the cross necklace through my T-shirt and ask God for forgiveness and protection. A good Christian woman with a healthy fear of God wouldn't have put herself here to dabble in the occult. I should've said "no" to coming. Yet, I didn't.

My head pounds. But there's no time to be sick. So I hustle to reach the others.

Bill, the news anchor, takes the offered key from the caretaker. He towers over us.

I guess that he's at least 6'2". His ocean blue eyes every once in awhile gleam with a hint of mischief. "Let's do this," he says as he twists the key into the padlock of the boarded-up double doors.

The lock clicks open. I brace myself against a bricked column, near a tumbleweed that settled on the porch. Everyone stands on the black floor tiles that proclaim "Goldfield Hotel." Some of the little squares had been gouged out.

The station's photographer films the procession crossing the threshold: the elderly caretaker who pats the doorframe as she enters; the psychic with her wavy long hair tied up in a gauzy scarf; her brother, the wiry veteran whose expertise is recording the voices of the dead; Janice; and the skeptical news producer who looks both ways as he steps into the building.

"Kathy." Bill holds open the heavy plywood-covered door for me.

I take a gulp of air. Try to smile. A little. It's not that I believe the hotel's really haunted. It's just I'm not convinced it can't be. And right at this moment, I know I'm not brave enough to say ghosts don't exist.

The past four years led me here. There must be a purpose to this. So why do I feel I'm standing on the precipice of disaster? I grip the doorjamb to steady myself.

God, please stay beside me.

~2~
Fragility

Sixteen years earlier, I attended a support group for those diagnosed with Chronic Fatigue Syndrome. No moderator, no counselor—just a group of us who participated in the U.S. Centers for Disease Control's Surveillance Study on CFS. The hospital conference room smelled of medicine and sterility.

We sat around a long rectangular table in a dark gray room with no artwork. I slouched and leaned my head against the chair back. A 20-year-old girl, wearing stylish clothes and the saddest expression I'd ever seen, sat next to me. At least I'd had most of my 20s to live until CFS had clobbered me when I was 28. Seated on my other side, a wife tended to her gray-haired husband in an electric wheelchair. Sick for more than seven years, his weakness was so progressed, he had difficulty talking, so his wife translated his mumbling.

"Jack feels hopeful. He started treatments in Mexico. His mind's improving and he's regaining some of his strength." She pulled out a water bottle, flipped the top and handed it to Jack, helping him guide the drink to his mouth.

A middle-aged man with a sour expression and unshaven face spoke up. "Jack always tries something new. Jack always has hope. When's he gonna realize he'll never get better? Maybe his life would be easier if he drops his high expectations and accepts it as it is."

"How dare you?" I responded, my anger fueling a short adrenaline burst. "How dare you find fault in someone who wants to live a better life? I respect Jack for never giving up. For his strength. Who are you to say he'll never get better? You are not God."

The man shook his chubby finger at me from across the conference table. He spat his words at me. "Neither are you. And you're just like Jack. You look at everything so rosy. People we know are taking their lives. They can't cope. We live in hell. You need to wake up as well, missy."

My head pounded to the thumping of my pulse. I had to lie down. I couldn't believe I'd wasted my precious energy to come to this stupid group. I prayed I could hold on to my defense before my brain misfired. "There's a reason we're all going through this. One day, I'll get better. I can't give up…and you know what? I'd rather be like Jack than like you."

Someone clapped. Another laughed. But what I heard next struck me down. "Get a clue. Nothing good can come out of this. You'll never get better." My mind short circuited. I looked around the room blankly. I didn't know who'd said it. I didn't even know if it was a man or woman.

"This is no support group," I murmured. With all the strength I could summon, I pushed back my chair and stumbled away from the table using my hands to steady me as I hurried out into the hall. Crying, I flopped down on an orange, padded bench and curled up in the fetal position. I was so weak I didn't know if I could get to my car, let alone drive home. My body melted into the cushions; I couldn't tell where the vinyl ended and my body began.

The young woman who'd sat next to me came out with my purse. "You left this inside." She sat next to me. "You're right, you know. Don't listen to them. We are all going to get better. We just have to."

Somehow, I managed to get myself home.

Two years ago my doctor had proclaimed I'd be back to work in a year. That hadn't happened. My health declined at a frightening speed. My neurologist told me my brain didn't have the energy to function correctly. My body couldn't regulate its temperature. My blood pressure remained dizzyingly low. And I was incapable of sleeping more than 2 to 3 hours each night. I didn't have the mental ability to read the breeziest of novels, and I couldn't rely on my eyes to function well enough to show me consistently what was there.

With my savings long gone, I earned little selling cosmetics and writing an occasional article for a patient editor who gave me three months to write a 500-word story that had once taken me three hours to complete. My credit card debt mounted.

I took charge of my health, no longer relying on physicians who wouldn't take me seriously. I went to clinics. Homeopaths. An Oriental doctor of medicine. Physical therapy. I'd even traveled to Johns Hopkins to participate in a research study, but was rejected.

My faith in God sustained me through the darkest days of this illness. I prayed and studied the Bible during the brief periods when I could read. God was with me. I knew my Lord wouldn't leave. And only the Almighty knew the purpose this illness would play in my life.

One early spring afternoon, I left my doctor's office and drove the fast lane of the McCarran Boulevard ring road toward home. I was especially weak; I needed to get to bed. A DJ prattled on the radio, breaking my concentration. I turned both him and the radio off.

The doctor had had nothing new to say. Perhaps I should have just stopped wasting my money and energy going to him. I swallowed 36 prescription pills a day, more than my 93-year-old grandmother took. Besides taking the edge off my pervasive pain, the medications didn't help.

I breezed through the intersection with Virginia Street. The traffic was sparse as everyone was at work. Except for me. I didn't remember what it was like to feel well enough to hold a job. I wondered if any employees out there realized how fortunate they were to work. How great it was to be productive, to contribute to a whole. To matter.

Suddenly, I slammed on the brakes as if to avoid hitting something. My seatbelt jerked me back into my seat. I looked around.

Nothing was there. No obstacles. No drivers. No stop sign.

My Honda CRX and I sat motionless in the fast lane. My mind mired in a fog. *Why did I stop?* I wasn't at an intersection. Nothing had crossed the road. But there I was motionless in the fast lane of a major Reno artery.

I stepped on the gas and pulled into the slow lane. I couldn't shift, accelerate and steer at the same time. It confounded me. How had I managed this all before? I drove home in second gear at 15 miles an hour, concentrating on keeping my car in its lane.

I'd never realized driving required so much minutiae, that is, until that moment. So overwhelming. I kept moving the steering wheel a little to the left, a little to the right. *Press the gas down more. Let it up. Brake.* No thought or action flowed automatically; every little movement required my complete attention.

Life had punched me in the stomach. I wanted to vomit. I needed to be able to drive.

A red car passed. I held my breath, hoping nothing went wrong while I stared at the white dotted line that separated us.

Near the left turn onto Baring Boulevard, I kept steering. *Hit the turn indicator. Check my mirrors. Slowly get into the fast lane, then the turn lane. Down shift. Stop.* The turn indicator beeps struck me as deafening. I stared at the red light, afraid I'd miss the green. My legs felt likely to collapse. The effort to hold down the brake and clutch seemed too big a job for them to manage.

"God, please get me home. Clear my brain. Let it function. Help me retain enough driving knowledge to get me the last bit home."

Finally, I pulled into the condo parking lot and, with great effort, managed to park my Honda. I cut the engine and set the parking brake. "Shit!" I yelled and dropped my head on the steering wheel. This had never happened before. No matter how sick I'd been, I could drive.

It was hell to have enough mental capacity to know that my faculties were eroding. The bile rose to my throat.

Oh Lord, I have to be able to drive. I HAVE TO. If I can't, my last thread of independence dies. I gripped the wheel with both hands until they hurt.

Disease prohibited me from participating in everyday life. No longer could I keep the condo clean or even pay for it. And even though we weren't married, Ken—my significant other of 14 years—had moved in to help support me. I'd never thought I'd live in sin with a man. Or let my parents pay my mortgage for that matter.

I have to get to the doctor. To the grocery store. I have to be able to drive. To escape.

"What's the point of fighting this if both my brain and body continually let me down?" I cried aloud, and then listened just in case God wanted to answer me. But there was no reply. Just the clinking from the motor cooling off.

I hoisted my worthless body out of the car. But instead of walking alongside my building to the stairwell and my unit, I turned and plodded diagonally toward the traffic light one block away. It was if I was on autopilot. I didn't know why I walked in that direction, but that didn't stop me. I trudged across the small parking lot.

My legs wobbled and I stumbled over my lousy feet. I stopped. I needed to go to bed. I couldn't sit down on the red curb, as I lacked the strength to get back up. Fighting this disease wasn't worth it. I couldn't do anything. I was nothing.

"This isn't a life," I grumbled, out of breath from the exertion of walking. I'd been a lump that spent every day in bed gazing out the window at the clouds drifting by, or reclining on the couch, watching bad daytime TV. I could barely sit up long enough to eat a meal, let alone shower.

My skull pounded. I paused at the curb of the parking lot and slowly lifted my foot up to reach the top of the cement. I heaved my body up and lugged myself across the greening-up lawn.

There was the signal. The intersection. I turned back and looked at my condo, pale yellow like the rest. The condo I'd purchased in my 20s. When life had been full of dreams. Now, it was just a nightmare.

Winded, I couldn't get enough oxygen no matter how deeply I inhaled. My muscles didn't want to move; they were like stone, unyielding, inflexible.

Cars sped through the intersection. I pushed forward, willing my legs to move, to resist the gravity. Step by step.

I made it. I leaned against the signal pole as the cross traffic got a green light.

Cars passed me by. Life passed me by. Two people in a silver car laughed. Lived. Drove.

Down the bend near the large cottonwood where the red-tail hawk normally perched, a semi approached. A truck driving far too fast for that stretch.

Should I step off the curb onto the semi's path? End it all. Quickly.

Quit being a burden to my parents, Ken and everyone else. I'd be free of pain. Death would be relief.

Perhaps people would've thought it an accident. After all, there wasn't a suicide note.

Just a few more steps. I can end this. Be free of this deteriorating body and mind.

The semi rapidly approached. There was still time if I acted right away. I leaned out toward the street. Took one step. And another. My toes hung over the curb.

I froze. Paralyzed. The semi sped past me, the force of its wind pushing my limp body back to the signal pole. I hugged the cold, steel pillar and cried. Never in my life had I thought I could've seriously considered ending my life.

That night, I lay in bed and tried to relax my exhausted, sleep-deprived body in preparation for a long, sleepless night. Then a strange sensation. One that I wasn't alone. I turned over. At the side of my bed, a dark patch appeared, one that made no sense. Nothing was around to cast a shadow and my unit was on the second floor, so no one could walk by my window.

Were my eyes playing tricks on me?

No. Because I became immersed in immense love. Sadness. And a voice played like music in my mind.

"Don't do what I did, Kathy. Don't do what I did." The blackness dissolved. Gone. And so was the sensation of love mixed with sadness.

I gasped, putting my hand to my heart. I knew who that was. My Uncle Allan! He'd committed suicide my junior year in high school. Allan had come to me! God had sent one of my favorite uncles to save me!

~3~
Seeking God's Acceptance

Since I can remember, I've *known God exists.*

From time to time as a child, I'd regularly feel The Great I Am's presence. It'd sneak up on me unexpectedly; I could've been making mud pies, reading *Fun with Dick and Jane*, playing tetherball or even drying dishes for Mom when I knew the Lord had arrived. This divine presence would announce itself the same way: an intensity of love tingling at the crown of my head, then migrating down my body—a kind of electrically charged hug turning me into one large smile. When this sensation of warm, happy fullness would appear, I'd lock on to this feeling, savoring it, as it never lasted longer than a few minutes. But while the tingling would subside, the unique afterglow of love—one stronger than the adoration of a hundred doting parents—stayed with me through the day.

I'd picture God in blinding brilliance, gazing at me in my twin braids, not-grown-into-ears and gangly body. And I realized the Being That Matters Most completely accepted me.

Acceptance, though, didn't come easily from my peers. I never really fit in. In school, I'd hover at the periphery, not quite an outcast, not really normal. Despite this, at every point of my youth, I had at least one good friend who accepted my strong predisposition to behave. For once I *knew* God was nearby, I did all I could to obey every rule. And I'd tell others they should obey them as well. I was the girl who routinely helped the teacher and befriended the outcast with the crusty orifices. Who avoided the back of the schoolyard where the sixth graders made it to second and third base though they never neared the ball field. I was the teen who had no interest in partying. And didn't ditch class. Ever.

I assumed everyone experienced God as I did. And it baffled me they made no efforts to please the Almighty. God watched me, visited me. And I was determined to make my Lord proud of me.

My parents—generous with time, love and attention for my little brother and me—never pushed religion. We were Methodists, but only attended church on sporadic Sundays, especially once we were old enough to take part in secular activities. My family had much to do on weekends: working around the house; spending time at our white and salmon-colored singlewide trailer on the Colorado River (our getaway from the crowds and suffocating smog of L.A.); or exploring historical sites and museums during fun day outings. I loved family time, never giving thought to my parents' lukewarm response to religion.

So occasionally, I sought out church to fill my spiritual yearnings. I tagged along with friends to their various congregations: Lutheran, Unitarian, Catholic, Jehovah's Witnesses and Latter Day Saints. To revel in the songs, the stained glass. To invite Him to visit me more often.

In college, I became a Born Again Christian and was obsessed with trying to save my loved ones. *They needed to confess Jesus as their savior or they'd go to hell.* Each night, I prayed for their souls, knowing if I talked to them about my beliefs, they'd close tightly like clamshells. So I never addressed my conversion to them directly. Instead, I hoped they'd note my regular participation in the New Life Assembly of God and my new sense of inner peace.

Unfortunately, an absolute conceit grew within me from knowing I'd be going to heaven and others were destined for hell. It placed me above them, those who were clueless enough to eschew Born Again Christianity.

Insidiously—without consciously realizing it—I judged others. For not being Born Again. For not studying the Bible. For living sinful lifestyles devoid of God. At the time, I never saw any of this as judging. I thought of it as love. But in my conviction of my own eternity, of believing I was right and all others were wrong, I judged myself into a box, a rigidity God would've never condoned.

One such time occurred in 2000 when my best friend Bonnie confided that she'd sought a psychic's advice. I called her un-Christian and told her she was playing with the devil. I couldn't believe she was condemning herself. She knew better.

At the friend's trailer we were visiting, Bonnie washed up in the bathroom next door, while I sat up in bed. She switched the topic from her visiting a psychic to my upcoming neurosurgery.

"I hope it's the answer," Bonnie said as the water ran in the sink. "I can't imagine how bad it's been for you this past decade. Is your herniated brain causing your CFS and that weird nerve disease?"

"The neurosurgeon says it isn't. He thinks it'll take care of some of my problems: the dizziness, the all-over headaches and my inability to bend over. But I'm hoping the surgery will do more. I really believe it could be the answer."

"Gosh, wouldn't that be great! I sure hope you're right, but why do you think it will do more than the surgeon thinks it will?"

"Just a hunch, I guess. I'm really praying for this. To feel like myself again. If this doesn't work, I don't know what to try next."

"Then I'll pray this surgery takes care of everything," Bonnie said.

I heard her brush her teeth.

I turned out the bedside lamp and pulled the covers to my shoulders as I stayed upright. The light from her bathroom spilled into the hall.

Then without a noise, they appeared in the doorway. Two dark shadows—one of a man, the other, a woman.

I blinked my eyes as if I could clear them away. *What are they?*

Bonnie turned the faucet off. I heard a drawer open and shut.

I froze, transfixed on these strange shadows as they slowly approached me. Specters darker than the night. I couldn't move. Talk. Or even look away. It was definitely two people—without tangible bodies. The woman was shorter than the man, and thick-waisted. The man was thin. For some reason, I believed they were much older than I was even though I couldn't see any details—just black forms. They came nearer to me with each passing second.

This can't be happening.

Bonnie said something, but her voice became background.

The couple was so near, I could almost touch them. And they were still heading my way.

What do they want with me?

I had to do something. I gathered my wits. And screamed.

Bonnie ran into the room as the couple vanished.

"What's the matter?" She flipped on the overhead light.

I was trembling. "I, I saw something."

"What do you mean, something?" Her face shone white from the night cream she hadn't rubbed in yet.

"A man and a woman. At least, I think it was a man and a woman. They came toward me." I sounded insane even to myself.

She gave me a puzzled, worried look. "I didn't hear anything. Are you thinking they broke in?"

I could tell by her face that she thought it implausible. She stepped into the hall, looked both ways, then returned.

I sank into the bed and drew up the blankets to my chin. "No. They didn't break in. I don't know. Maybe they weren't real." A deep cold penetrated my bones.

"Wait here." She pivoted on her heel and ran out of the room. I heard the methodical clicks, thuds of Bonnie checking the doors, windows.

My heart pounded. *What's wrong with me? Did I really see them?*

She returned. "Everything's locked. No one's here except for us. Could you have fallen asleep and had a nightmare?"

My eyes narrowed. *It hadn't been a nightmare.* My sudden conviction surprised me. "No. I was listening to you brushing your teeth. I hadn't even lain down yet."

"Oh. OK. How about…now—don't take this wrong—but does the doctor have you on anything that could possibly make you hallucinate?"

I mentally went over the list of medications I was taking. A lot of anti-inflammatories. Neurological drugs. "I don't think so," I said, not quite convinced.

"Perhaps you overdid it today." She came over and sat on the bed. "We shouldn't have taken a walk. We should've stayed inside."

"I needed fresh air. We were out for, what, ten minutes? And we only stood for half the time."

"There really isn't any other explanation," Bonnie said. "Unless you think they were ghosts." She smiled just a bit.

"NO! I'm not saying that." I exhaled loudly. "Maybe you're right. I don't know. Let's just go to sleep."

"OK. Holler if you need anything." She turned off my light.

I lay there for hours, keeping my eyes shut tightly. I had seen something. Something not of this world. But ghosts didn't exist. And my medications had never caused anything like that before. Perhaps I'd experienced some strange, cognitive lapse? I wasn't sure what was better to hope for, that my poor health could make me hallucinate or I was witnessing things that weren't supposed to exist.

~4~
Ghost Hunter

I held the pink Post-It scrawled with the ghost hunter's name—Janice Oberding, her phone number and 2 p.m., the time of our appointment that day. I pressed it back onto the edge of my computer monitor as if I could forget about it. Even on my worst cognitive day, I couldn't forget my first meeting with a ghost buster!

In my office, which doubled as the department storeroom, I gazed at the wall of cabinets wondering why someone would really choose to be in such a preposterous line of work. *Wasn't* Ghostbusters *a far-fetched comedy? Concentrate.*

My boss wanted me to publicize our newest class, but the interview was just ten minutes away and I had stared at the blank Word document for half an hour. *What do you ask someone like this?*

Ms. Oberding was scheduled to teach Ghost Hunting 101 for the continuing education division of Truckee Meadows Community College. And I needed to write a press release to gain media coverage so people would know we were offering the class.

My stomach fluttered, though I wasn't sure why. Obviously, my Christian beliefs cast a shadow of suspicion about her. But it was more. I thought of our angel class instructor. Of how different he had been. How I couldn't wait to get away from him.

I had met him while coordinating an open house to showcase the variety of courses we offered. Being new to the department, I'd made it a point to sit in for 10 minutes or so of each mini class to better understand the variety of programs we offered.

I'd sat far off to one side, so I wouldn't disrupt his presentation when I needed to leave. About 25 people had shuffled in and taken their places.

The tall, wiry instructor had cleared his throat. "Today you are going to gain a few tips on how to better communicate with your angels. We have angels around us all the time and they want to help us live better lives."

The students' heads had bobbed almost in unison. Personally, I'd doubted angels followed us around. Yeah, the Bible had mentioned a few instances—but those were extraordinary circumstances with outstanding people. I hadn't been one to buy into the guardian angel business, a crutch used by the weak-minded.

"You have power. A lot of power." He'd paused and looked about the room. "You are God. Each and every one of you are gods."

It had felt like an ant army marched across my skin. *Did I hear him say we were Gods? How arrogant. Offensive. There's only one real God.*

"The angels answer to you. They serve you. And—"

I'd bolted from the chair, exiting the classroom into the institutional green hallway. Leaning against the wall, I'd silently prayed for forgiveness for setting up this demonstration. In playing a role in corrupting the souls of others. Clearly, this instructor had been on the fast track to hell.

I realized it was unfair of me to judge Janice by one experience three years ago. After all, I hadn't met her yet. I had to stay focused. I wouldn't smile too smugly or make off-hand comments. It wasn't my place. Our division represented the community, so if people really wanted to turn in their hard-earned money to take such an odd class, it was their prerogative. My paycheck would remain in my wallet, thank you very much.

I pictured Janice looking kind of spooky with long flowing, black hair streaked with gray. Her eyes peering out from overdone makeup. And definitely wearing funky, Bohemian clothing accented with a breezy long scarf.

Running out of time, I typed basic questions I'd ask anyone and hope for on-the-spot inspiration.

My palms sweated, even though I hadn't been able to get my body to warm up all day. I slipped on a sweater and wiped my palms on my wool business skirt as Humberto, a coworker, appeared at my door.

"Janice Oberding's here to see you." He gestured to the woman behind him. She looked like someone's young grandmother. Not a ghost hunter.

"Hi." She took my hand, shook it firmly. "So nice to meet you, Kathy."

I smiled and swung my still-moist palm to the metal chair beside my 1950s surplus desk. The small movement burned all the muscles in my arm. "Nice to meet you."

She appeared so normal in a conservative, navy business suit and 2-inch, closed-toe pumps. Her wavy, reddish-brown hair looked as if she fought it to behave, even though it had been cut short. Red lipstick, which worked on her, punctuated her subdued makeup. Dimples flanked her warm smile. Part of me was disappointed; part was relieved. But I kept my guard up. The angel teacher had appeared normal as well.

"Why don't we just jump right into this interview, okay?" I said.

"Of course." She sat her mid-sized leather purse on the floor next to the chair.

"How did you get into this line of work?"

"I've believed in ghosts since I was a child. I've also been equally interested in history." She leaned toward me. "My take as a paranormal investigator's a bit different from the average ghost hunter. You see, what I like to do is find the tie-in—why a place may be haunted by investigating the history behind the location. I'm just curious by nature. I love combing old newspaper articles, court records and such. It's so exciting when I find a connection: the reason behind a haunting." The words tumbled out her crimson lips. Her passion for this subject sparkled in her hazel eyes. She folded her hands on her lap.

I finished typing my notes into the computer.

"Are you a writer?" she asked.

"Yes, for as long as I can remember."

She nodded. "So you must understand what I'm saying. About curiosity and wanting to learn more. All writers are inquisitive by nature."

"Yes. I do." I returned her smile. My breathing slowed to normal. My shoulders relaxed.

Janice continued. "You know what I think? Who cares if there's a ghost. The question is WHY is there a ghost?"

"You mean why would a place be haunted? OK. Why?" I asked.

"The spirits have unfinished business. An unresolved issue or feeling of injustice. Take this story about a murdered nurse in Chicago. The police have no leads. Years later, this dead nurse visits a good friend. Telling her things only the murder victim would know. See? She wanted justice! Or perhaps, a ghost's someone who died unexpectedly and doesn't know she's dead and should move on. Or maybe, she has fond memories of a place and enjoys being there."

"Interesting," I said automatically as my fingers quickly pecked at the keyboard. I went to the next question on my list. "What are your qualifications to teach this class?"

"I'm a certified ghost hunter and a member of the American Ghost Hunting Society."

There are enough of you out there for a society? I stopped typing. *Focus on the interview.* "How do you get certified?" *Spend the night in a haunted house? Read Stephen King? Don't judge her. She's nice.*

"I took classes. I learned techniques. I found how perfectly logical happenings may appear to be paranormal, but in reality, they're not. I can better pick out a hoax than most people. You know, there's a movement to make this profession more legitimate by objectively looking at the evidence. There are times when you have to say, 'No. That's not a ghost.' But there are instances I can't explain away." Her eyes wandered over my space to the mannequin snugged between a stack of boxes and the corner. "We've got company I see." She laughed.

Most people felt startled when they saw him, but it hadn't fazed her in the least. "Janice, meet Biff. My roommate. We use him in our window displays." I found I liked her. Her warmness. Passion. And professionalism.

"Ah." She turned back to me. "For most of us, if we are truly honest with ourselves, we know we've had experiences that cannot be logically solved. As a society, we blame incidents on our imagination. What happens if we stop discounting and start paying attention to these episodes?" Her gaze grew intense.

I swore she stared into my soul. My eyes locked on hers. I did have a great imagination. There was nothing wrong with being creative. I glanced away and shuffled a small pile of papers on my desk as if I had been looking for something. I needed to maintain a professional distance.

If Janice noted my hesitation, she didn't mention it. "Let me tell you a story. A while back, my family and I stayed at the Mizpah. You know the hotel in Tonopah?"

I nodded and resumed typing more out of wariness than to get down the information.

"We were leaving the hotel room when, all of a sudden, we saw a green mist float from one side of the hall to the other. Just floating." Her hands made a wave-like pattern in the air. "My whole family saw it. I've gone over this repeatedly, and even after the seminars I've attended, I still can't explain why all of us would see it. I believe it had to be paranormal."

"Weren't you scared?" I couldn't imagine what I'd do if I saw a hovering green mist. Actually, yes I could. I'd scream and run the other way. Then I chided myself. *Ghosts do not exist.*

"No, I wasn't. You have to understand, ghosts aren't the way Hollywood portrays them. The reality's not exciting enough to be a movie. If a ghost was a nice person in life, it'll be a nice spirit. If it was a negative person, then it'll be a negative entity. Most ghosts are fine."

I couldn't fathom how she could talk about the paranormal so matter-of-factly. "So blood doesn't drip from the walls, and they can't reach out and strangle you?" I laughed and, even to myself, I sounded a bit uneasy.

"Right. That's all Hollywood....And whether you believe in ghosts or not is your own personal matter. I'm not here to convince anyone. I want to help those who do believe. Who may be frightened. I want them to know they needn't be."

I'd always believed those who dabbled in the black arts—and it seemed to me seeking out ghosts fell into that category—tantalized Satan. Yet she hadn't proselytized, hadn't tried to drag me over to the dark side. She'd acknowledged there were hoaxes. And, my skin didn't crawl as it did with the angel teacher.

With the interview concluded, I walked her to the front desk, marveling that I really did like her.

◆   ◆   ◆

The press picked up our story and Ghost Hunting 101 filled even after moving it to a classroom twice its size. After reviewing the overwhelmingly positive class evaluation forms, my boss expanded the course into a full-blown ghost hunting conference set for October 2003.

Writing the copy for the ghost conference brochure, I took a lighthearted approach. "Hear tales of things that go bump in the night," and so on. The graphic artist used a cartoon ghost font called PhilliBoo. It never occurred to me anyone would really take this subject seriously.

Startlingly white, pillow clouds floated through the lapis Nevada sky as my boss, Janice and I spent the afternoon in the not-quite-dead ghost town of Virginia City. We were there to prepare for the paranormal investigation portion of the ghost conference.

Virginia City, located 20 or so miles southeast of Reno, brimmed with souvenir shops, candy stores and strange little businesses, such as the Red Light Museum that was dedicated to the city's once thriving prostitution industry. In the 1870s, this community—built upon a wealth of silver ore—had been one of the most significant towns between Denver and San Francisco. This day, Victorian mansions clung to the hillsides above C Street, the main drag. Below were smaller, white clapboard houses in various stages of dilapidation. A history buff myself, I had periodically visited "VC" as we locals called it. I'd strolled the boardwalks, imagining the miners, the wealthy and the ladies of the night who'd traveled these same paths more than one hundred and twenty years ago.

We pulled into the long driveway of the St. Mary's Arts Center, a stately, three-story brick mansion sporting a columned porch. This serene locale had spent much of its early life as Virginia City's only hospital and orphanage.

Janice rapped on the locked double doors. No one answered.

"I'll go to the back and see if anyone's around," my boss said.

She descended the steps, then disappeared behind the building.

St. Mary's Arts Center. Photo by Kathleen Berry.

My legs felt burdened by invisible, massive lead weights that dragged me down with each step. I sat down on one of the porch's wicker chairs and gazed up the hill at downtown VC. I wished I didn't have to contend with my illness today. I would've loved to go just one day without pain and weakness.

There was an easy silence between Janice and me. We'd met numerous times planning the conference and I'd grown to enjoy her company.

Janice softly cleared her throat. "Kathy, I'm curious. Do you feel anything?"

Maybe my brain misfired, as her question made no sense to me. But instead of asking her to elaborate, I just winged it. "Everything's fine. It's a pretty day and I'm not in the office, so what can I complain about?"

"Yes, it's nice out...I mean, do you feel anything about this place?"

"What?"

Janice looked to where my boss had disappeared. "I want to know if you sense anything strange about this place. If you think someone's staring at you, but no one's there. Or if your emotions quickly change.

Let me know if you intuit *anything* about this place, okay?"

I didn't know what she was getting at.

"Kathy, I believe you can sense spirits."

My eyes widened. I didn't want to disappoint Janice, but I wasn't one of *those* people. I worked to keep my voice upbeat, positive, so I wouldn't insult her. "Thanks for the vote of confidence, but I'm not psychic. Why would you think that?"

She smiled. "I'm a good judge of people when it comes to things like this. And I've got a hunch about you. Do me a favor, okay? Stay open to possibilities. Pay attention to those nagging little feelings you may get. Don't explain everything away. You may be surprised at what you're capable of."

I shook my head. "I really don't think I'm psychic, Janice." *I am a Christian. Not a fortuneteller. I don't read minds, see auras or talk to the dead*. I hoisted myself off the chair and walked to the edge of the porch. "I wonder where the manager is. I sure hope we can get in today."

"Oh, I'm sure she's around," Janice said.

I leaned against the porch rail, closed my eyes and absorbed the sun's rays. *No. I'm not psychic. Janice thinks she's giving me a compliment. Take it and move on.*

My boss returned with the manager, who gave us a brief tour of the building except for the closed-off third floor. Various types of artwork, created by the center's teachers, dotted the walls of the off-white, high-ceilinged hallways. Most rooms were small, holding only a twin bed or two. The communal bathrooms were located down the hall. The manager told us some of their students had said it was haunted there. However, she didn't believe in such nonsense.

Janice winked at me.

The phone rang and the manager excused herself. We wandered about on our own. I sensed nothing, and I was glad for that. *Janice is wrong.*

My boss ducked into a room, leaving Janice and me alone once again.

"Why don't we go into the basement?" Janice said.

"Why not?"

We crept down the stairs. All was still except for our footfalls. At the base of the steps where a bunch of junk—old dusty wood chairs, frames, boxes—was stored, I got a chill up my spine. I stopped. Looked behind me. Nothing was there. Still, I couldn't shake the sensation that someone watched me. I turned back toward Janice hoping she didn't notice my hesitation. No such luck.

"What's the matter?"

She's making me paranoid. "Something may be watching me right now." I sounded just plain silly and regretted saying it. *She planted this stupid psychic notion in my brain. Nothing's there.*

"Good!" she smiled. "I have a suggestion, if you're willing to try it. In the next few weeks, think of the odd instances that have happened in your life. The things you've discounted. Situations you've found no rational explanations for. And—now, listen to me—having an imagination isn't a good enough reason."

"But. Nothing's there. Really…Probably a draft…Maybe paranoia."

"Kathy, trust yourself." She placed her hand on my arm. "Listen to your intuition. I bet you'll realize things have been happening to you all along, but you've pushed them down, deep inside so you wouldn't have to deal with them."

I stared at her. I didn't have a reply. *And I don't want to think about what she's saying.* "Let's go upstairs. They're probably looking for us."

~5~
Memories

I curled up on the couch with my Bible, trying to dislodge Janice's words from my mind. *I can't be psychic. I just can't be. She must be wrong.* The Old Testament was clear about those types of things. I opened my New International Version edition to find where it covered the evils of psychics and such.

Isaiah 8:19—*When men tell you to consult mediums and spiritists, whisper and mutter, should not a people inquire of their God? Why consult the dead on behalf of the living?"*

I'd never sought out a psychic or medium—but it didn't address being a psychic. Next entry.

Deuteronomy 17:10—*Let no one be found among you who…is a medium or spiritist who consults the dead. Anyone who does these things is detestable to the Lord…."*

Just great. How could this have applied to me? I'd been a good Christian. I studied the Word nightly. I prayed for discernment. I tried to live an exemplary life for the Almighty. And I adhered to the Golden Rule.

Janice had said I should think about strange incidents that had happened in my life. As much as I fought the urge to do so, I couldn't stop the unbidden images. I lifted myself off the couch and walked out on our condo balcony as the desert foothills turned orange. And I recalled something I hadn't thought about since I had been a toddler.

I wake up screaming, struggling to catch my breath. The room soundless, black, except for a streetlight's soft glow just touching my bedroom window. We live in a duplex near the Santa Anita Racetrack in Monrovia, California.

They're here again, crowding around my crib. The solid dark shapes of full-sized animals—giraffe, lion, bear, horse—and the shadow of a man wearing a top hat. It's like a circus act, yet I'm the one in the cage, made of the crib's slatted sides, which they come to see. Watching me. Watching me. Watching me.

My heart thumps so loudly, I'm afraid they can hear it.

Mommy always says it's just a bad dream. Nothing's there. She's wrong. My bed's too small. If only I could get a big girl's bed, they wouldn't be able to get so close. I'd curl up in the center of the mattress, protected. Until then, I pull the covers over my head and hope they'll go away. Or maybe since I can't see them under my blankets, they won't see me and they'll forget I'm here.

But even in my young toddler brain, I know it's wishful thinking for they visit regularly. Returning just to watch me and nothing else. Once we move to a new house, it stops. They don't follow me to our new home.

Surely, this had been my imagination. Perhaps it'd been a nightmare, though the intensity of fear and anxiety return as if it had happened yesterday, not 40-plus years ago.

The normally drab hills looked beautiful, bathed in the deepening glow of the waning sun. I leaned against the banister. And another memory from a time before I fell ill crowded my consciousness.

I'm the publicist for the Reno-Sparks Convention and Visitors' Authority. It's the night before the Festival of Trees press conference. I'm holding it in Reno's oldest residence, the Lake Mansion, whose upstairs also houses our offices. The foundation that owns the two-story, white wooden building with a mansard roof has given me permission to hold this media event here on two conditions: no food or drink can be served in the parlor, and I'm to remove the smaller antiques and, once the event is over, return them to their exact places.

My coworkers say this place is haunted. They've heard something unseen storm up the staircase. They've even watched the front door rattle as someone pounded on it, but once opened, the shadowy figure vanished along with any footprints in the freshly fallen snow. Nothing's happened to me, though, so I don't mind when the janitors pack up for the night and leave me alone to finish.

I've created a room map to record where all the smaller antiques and trinkets belong. I carefully pick up porcelain figurines, beautiful antique vases and historic photos, placing them on the bed in a nearby closed-off room. I remove two small tapestry-covered chairs as well. Before I leave for the night, I place the map in my desk's left-hand drawer, so I won't lose it.

The next morning, I arrive at 6:30 a.m.—well before my coworkers— to set up the chairs, podium and such. I unlock the double wooden doors and step inside.

Something's amiss. It takes me a moment to realize why. All the dozens of small antiques have returned to the parlor. I walk the room in a confused state, and then run to the bedroom where I had put them. Nothing's on the mattress; the white knotty bedspread—smooth as if it had just been made—looks untouched. I run upstairs and grab the map from the drawer and go back down. Everything, including the chairs, has been put back in the same exact places!

I call our janitorial staff. They say they didn't return. Could this be a practical joke? I doubt it, as no one—except for Myron Lake's great grandson—would know where each piece goes.

I shivered. Okay, that could prove ghosts exist. Perhaps. But if they'd moved things around when I wasn't there, that was no indication I was psychic.

The hills had become silhouettes against a royal purple sky.

My brain continued scanning my memories. As much as I would have liked to, I couldn't turn it off.

This time, I travelled back 15 years.

I slide the raffle ticket along with a $50 check into the pre-printed envelope to the African Fund for Endangered Wildlife. We came home from our safari only two weeks ago, and AFEW's grand prize is an all-expense paid, private tour of Kenya for two. Although I'm still sick with this lousy African flu, I want to go back. I lick the stamp, affix it and set the envelope next to my purse by the front door.

Ken goes home early, so I can get to bed. It's only 8 p.m., but I go to bed any way. I lay there for hours, awake—only moving when the pain grows so fierce throughout my body, I need to change positions and exert myself to turn over. At 11:12 p.m., my neighbor pulls into the carport and stomps up his stairs. I'm still awake at 1:27 a.m., when my other neighbor gets home from working in the casino pits. Her dog barks as she hurries down the sidewalk.

"AGH! I've got to sleep. I can't take this anymore. Oh, Lord, help me. I can't get over this flu unless I get some rest. Please help me," I whisper.

It's 3 a.m. and I'm more alert than when I first went to bed. My alarm's to go off at 6:15. I push the frustration from my mind by concentrating on a relaxation technique. I curl up my toes. Release them. Tighten my arches. Release. Flex my ankles. Relax....By the time I'm tightening my shoulders, I drift off. And dream.

"You want to take another three-week vacation?" My normally understanding boss looks at me sternly from behind her expansive desk. "You're only entitled to a two-week vacation once a year. I gave you an extra week off just five months ago."

I wring my hands. I love my job so much. "But I won this all-expense paid African safari. I can't turn it down."

"This is our busy season. Your leaving will make it difficult for your co-workers." She taps her fountain pen on a pad of paper. "I'm afraid you've left me no choice."

Buuuuzzzzzzz! My alarm clock sounds. Stretching in bed, I can't shake the vividness of this dream. Then with a certainty that roots deep within me, I realize I've won the raffle even though I haven't put it in the mail yet. No matter how much I argue the implausibility of this with myself, I know I'll win that safari.

I get up, secure the ticket stub on the fridge door with a magnet and wait for March 15, the drawing date.

Even though my illness spirals out of control, the pull of the continent is strong within me. Each day, I daydream of Africa's kind-spirited people, the rugged beauty of the Great Rift Valley and savannas, and the amazing wildlife. Winning this trip becomes a lifeline, a way to endure my worsening health.

March 15 finally arrives and there's no word from AFEW. I can't fathom that I didn't win the trip.

The next morning, I'm leaving for work when the phone rings.

"Is this Kathleen Berry?" a man asks.

"Yes."

"Hi, I'm from the African Fund for Endangered Wildlife. You entered our raffle for the private safari…"

I scream.

"I guess you've figured out you won."

I couldn't blame this incident on my imagination. The one time in my life I had had a premonition that came true. Okay. That one was irrefutable. But if I had been truly psychic, wouldn't this have happened more than once?

I guessed my dream about winning could've been a coincidence, strengthened by my desire to return to Africa.

The night had turned cold. Looking down, I could just make out the movements of someone walking a dog. I heard a voice. It was our neighbor walking her terrier, Reggie.

The lights came on in the different condos. I wrapped my sweater around me.

One more memory, this time from only a few years ago, pushed its way to the front of my recollections.

In 2001, a recurring dream—one steeped in rich, larger-than-life emotions of love and sadness—invades my sporadic sleep. Each time, the landscape's dark and rocky with looming black cliffs. Everything's black, white or gray. Except for my grandfather, who looks like he did most of my childhood. Bald, smelling subtly of pipe smoke and wearing a bluish-gray jumpsuit he'd wear whenever he tinkered in his workshop.

"I'm proud of you. You know that, right?" my deceased grandfather tells me.

"Yes. I do." I run to him and give him a big hug. He returns the embrace, his affection enveloping me. I'm no longer in bed, asleep. I've traveled somewhere distant, not of this world.

"I need you to help me. Tell your grandmother it's time for her to come to me."

Since I'm clinging to him, I can't see his face. But I can feel the warmth of his body. His request is not an easy one. I live in Nevada. Grandma lives in Texas.

"But Grandpa, I don't know how I'd do it. Grandma can't hear over the phone. And I can't write a letter. Aunt Sharron wouldn't appreciate me telling Grandma to die."

"Tell your grandmother I love her."

"But I don't have the money to travel. I have a lot of debt."

He gently pushes me back, but keeps his hands on my shoulders. His face is relaxed, smoother than I remember. "Tell your grandmother it's time for her to come back to me."

"But—"

"The time will soon be right. Please tell her."

I take his hands. I know he's getting ready to leave me. My sadness at his impending departure builds. "Grandpa, I miss you so much. Please don't go yet."

"I love you too." He disappears; my hands now grip the air. I wake up still carrying the strange mixture of all-encompassing love and grief. But the love, stronger than the grief, makes it just bearable for me.

This dream occurs three times.

Soon after, I get a call from my cousin Bryan, Great Aunt Ruby's son: "I'm afraid I have some bad news."

My hand clenches the phone. He's never called me before. "Is it your mom?"

"She's very bad. She asked for you. The doctors say it won't be much longer. Maybe two or three days. I thought you'd want to know."

Aunt Ruby and I clicked; she was more than a relative to me. We shared the same passions for family history and quilting. I respect this tough farmwoman full of common sense and strongly relying on ethics.

She beat cancer. Now she fights congestive heart failure. I guess I didn't really believe she would lose this battle.

So, I travel to Texas, say goodbye to my beloved aunt, and relay grandfather's message to my 95-year-old-grandma, who's bedridden and can't do much for herself. When I tell her what her husband said, she smiles and thanks me. I tell her my final goodbyes. I can see it on her face. She's going to listen to Grandpa.

She dies about a month later.

As I relived this memory with all its emotion, I knew this experience in no way could be construed as evil, ungodly. After all, my grandfather demonstrated love's endlessness. Grandpa had been in heaven. He had been right. It'd been time for my once strong-minded, feminist grandmother to find her wings. To rid herself of a deteriorating shell to be back with her soul mate once again. There was nothing evil in that.

However, just because my grandfather came to me in a dream didn't mean I was psychic.

My mind calmed down. No more memories raced forward. I sighed and returned inside. Everything was going to be okay. A few dreams, a coincidence and a little imagination. Hardly the stuff of psychics.

I thought of the Old Testament and how important my relationship with God was. I would not pursue this folly, this scree-covered slope where I could slide down into the abyss. I wasn't psychic. And I wasn't going to go to hell. That's all there was to it.

~6~
The Circus Master

Decked out in white lace and dolls, this room belied its use as the place for a deathbed. The stale air was thick with medicine and decay. Among the billowy sea of eyelet and pillows, a shrunken man sat propped up. George, my uncle, neared the end of his journey with prostate cancer.

He stared off, not realizing I'd arrived.

"Hi, George," I said a little too enthusiastically.

His thin, pale face slowly turned toward me. He smiled.

I entered the room, passing large dolls that stood on the floor like sentries. Their black glass, button eyes missed nothing.

How many men would've allowed their homes to be turned into frilly, feminine havens of girly childhood toys? Only George, who was confident in his masculinity and cognizant of his wife's less-than-ideal childhood.

With effort, he raised an arm to hug me hello. "Kathy." His whisper sounded more like a breath.

"George. I've come to see you." A stupid, obvious thing for me to say, but asking a dying man how he was doing just didn't seem right. I sat on the edge of the bed and leaned toward him. "Are they taking care of the pain?"

He nodded as I took his hand—it felt like bones in a sack—and held it loosely. His face was colorless and without his dentures, he looked one hundred and ten, instead of in the mid-80s. George had been a creator. A wiry, short man who had shaped wood into beautiful furniture.

He was whispering, and I couldn't make it out. "I'm sorry. Let me get closer. Can you tell me again?" My ear almost touched his lips as he started again.

"I…talked…to God."

I turned back to face him. "Really? What was that like?"

"Nice…I…talked…to God…about…you."

I looked about the room. If I caught his eyes, I'd sob. I lightly squeezed his hand, but gazed toward the curtained window. "Thank you so much. But you really need to talk to God about you. You need more divine help than I do." I sniffed. My eyes welled with tears. *Be strong. Look him in the eye.*

He shook his head. "I am…old…but you…you are young…I asked God…to take me…and to heal…you."

Tears ran down my cheeks. How could George fight for me when he was so sick? But this had always been George. Confident of himself and always, always thinking of others. Even-keeled. Kind. When I had fallen ill, languished in bed and wracked with pain, George had urged me to keep fighting. He'd even sent me a small check each month to help cover my living expenses while I'd been bedridden. How could I lose such a person, someone who always believed in me?

George took his free hand and painstakingly moved it to clasp my hands. "God…said…yes…he will…heal you." A tear ran down George's cheek.

I lost it. My vision blurred from the tears. Wetness tumbled down my face, and I tasted salt on my lips. "Thank you. Thank you." I kissed his moist cheek. My tears splashed against the white eyelet, temporarily creating little beige spots. "I really, really appreciate it. But, I wish, though, you had asked the Lord to heal you. You are the one who really needs it right now. I'm doing much better than the doctors ever said I would."

And I was. I could walk a mile at that time without stopping. I kept up with my 20 hour-a-week job. And once or twice a month, I'd conserved enough energy to do something fun—I wasn't confined to bed every minute once I'd gotten off work.

He shook his head. "My time…is here….God said…he would…heal you."

Oh, I hope you are right. Then I felt shame. Shame for dwelling on my situation and not on my dear uncle's. "I love you George. I love you so very much." I sniffed.

"I...love...you."

George died two days after our visit. Following his wishes, no funeral was held. News of his passing raised a mixture of feelings. Loss. Sadness. Relief that this man who never complained was finally free. Free of his body and with the Great I Am. I pressed on at work, occasionally tearing up, as I thought of how much I missed George.

Two weeks later, I lay in bed—it was a brisk night and my blankets and quilt reached to the base of my skull. My hand, refreshed in the chilly air, stuck out from the covers as I contemplated the next day's deadlines.

Then the strangest thing happened: someone grasped my hand. A subtle, yet distinct squeezing sensation. Affectionate. I lifted my head and glanced over. Ken was working in the Bay Area, so I was alone. No one was there, yet the feeling remained: a consistent, pleasant pressure. It hadn't occurred to me to be frightened. Instead, I experienced love and peacefulness. George came to mind and stayed there. I saw him inside my head, smiling, happy, healthy. I wasn't dreaming. My brain stayed clear, not foggy. With a growing certainty, I knew George held my hand. He was back. He was there to tell me he was all right.

I whispered, "Thank you, George. I miss you. Thank you for visiting me." Tears puddled on the pillow where my cheek rested. "I love you."

His grasp loosened, then released.

I pondered this. How I'd *known* it was George. How God had allowed my uncle to come down to convey he was fine. I couldn't say why I was so convinced this was George and not some weird muscle/hand contraction—it was just a knowing buried so deep within me, I would've betrayed George by not believing it.

At that moment, I recalled Janice's words: "Think about the strange incidents in your life that can't be explained away." This was certainly one of those, I was sure.

Mom and I drove north from Carson City to the Cattlemen's Restaurant to meet Dad for dinner. I loved the rugged bareness of Slide Mountain and how the thick forests of ponderosa met the meadows of the Washoe Valley. The sun neared setting as it painted the sky orange and brushed the clouds in pinks.

I needed to tell someone about George's visit and I'd decided to share it with Mom. I was nervous. After all, she was a practical, strong woman, who, in her sixties, could still dig up a sprinkler line and reinstall a new one. As soon as my little brother Craig had grown old enough for first grade, she had worked as a switchboard operator at the Broadway, a two-story department store near our home. Now, she was an assistant vice president for U.S. Bank, even though she never had earned a college degree. An intelligent and rational person. And more importantly, she wouldn't judge me.

My stomach roiled; the acid churned as it moaned. I was running out of time. We were almost there, so I plunged in. "Mom, George visited me the other night," I said as I tried to concentrate on the road.

"He did?" she asked placidly.

I'd expected her to find reasons to rationalize my experience, to tell me I was dreaming. She didn't.

I inhaled, not realizing I'd held my breath. "He came by and squeezed my hand when I was in bed, before I had a chance to fall asleep. It sounds funny, but I know it was him." I snatched a glimpse of my mother. Her defined cheekbones and dimples, dishwater brown hair and thin-lipped smile. The same features I shared with her.

Her expression was normal and calm. "He probably just wanted you to know he's okay. That's really nice."

I shook my head in disbelief. I'd hoped she'd take it well, but I'd never expected her to accept my news. It was if I had said something obvious like, "Mom, here's a stop sign. I think I'll brake." Then a revelation hit me. She must've had a similar experience. That's why she hadn't reacted. We passed the restored Winter's Mansion, a white two-story home nestled among the cottonwoods. "Mom, have you had experiences with someone who died? Did George visit you, too?"

"George hasn't visited me as far as I know, but I've had some strange experiences. You probably don't remember the duplex we lived in. You were so young then."

My heart beat faster. I clenched the steering wheel. "Actually, I do remember a few things about it. Like how my room's view was of a two-story apartment."

"Yes. You're right. I remember once waking in the middle of the night. I saw the clear outline of a man. He wore an old-fashioned hat and a suit. He stood at the foot of our bed. It was as if he were a dark shadow. It was the strangest thing," she said, as if musing.

I stared at her. My mouth hung open. She'd seen the Circus Master! I recalled my terror of the shadow animals and the tall man in the top hat who gathered around my crib. I'd convinced myself it was a nightmare, but dreams couldn't be shared.

My Camry straddled both northbound lanes. Mom didn't seem to notice. She'd time traveled 40 years, back to that duplex. Luckily, there wasn't anyone else driving near us, so I moved into the fast lane, then the turn lane. The oncoming traffic picked up and I had to wait for an opening to turn into the restaurant parking lot.

This can't be happening. If Mom saw him, he had to be real. I willed myself to sound calm and hoped the oncoming cars bought me enough time to finish this conversation. I spotted Mom's BMW parked next to the restaurant. Dad must've been inside. "Weren't you scared?"

"More startled. Your Dad was there asleep, so I wasn't really scared. I knew it wasn't a burglar. It wasn't human."

The turn signal beeped loudly. Or was it my heart pounding? "What did he look like?"

"He was tall and thin, I remember. And he was darker than the blackness of the room. He wasn't alive." She looked at me with her hazel eyes.

The congestion eased, but since no one was behind me, I acted as if I hadn't seen it. I hated making Dad wait, but I had to tell her.

"Oh Mom! I saw him, too! But in my room he showed up with a bunch of circus animals." While I shared all the details I could remember, Mom nodded. She told me she only remembered him visiting once, but the memory of it always had stayed with her. She didn't remember my toddler "nightmares." She'd never thought it would visit me as well.

I pulled the car into the parking lot. "Why didn't you ever tell me this?"

"I don't know. I haven't thought about it in years. Guess it never seemed important."

But on that day, its implication was staggering. Janice was right. I couldn't dismiss things that had happened as just my imagination. And with the knowledge of our shared psychic episodes, nothing would be the same from there on out. I could no longer deny that I had some kind of psychic ability. In sharing something Mom had kept to herself for almost forty years, she unlocked my past and blew open my future.

~7~
Shadowy Figure

It's happening again. Something had wakened me. *Stay calm.* I kept my eyes shuttered and grasped my sheets, pulling them over my head like a three year old scared of the Boogeyman.

I assessed the situation. Ken wasn't stirring in his room, and the neighbors were silent as well. A dog's distant serenade floated through the still night. Hardly loud enough to have wakened me from slumber.

I trembled. Someone was watching me. It was him. I knew it. He'd returned. I felt his gaze.

My heart raced. *This is ridiculous!*

Perhaps it was all in my mind. Maybe I'd thought he was here because he hadn't appeared in days. I wondered if I'd get used to that shadow man if he'd show up every night. I'd expect him and not get startled. There was a chance, I'd get used to it. *No.* That couldn't happen. Ever. I needed to get through the fright. Hiding didn't help; it only prolonged my horror.

Tugging the sheet off my face, I slowly opened my eyes and leaned toward the clock: 2:12 a.m. I sneaked a quick glance at the right side of the bed. *Good.* No one was there. Just the black void of the bathroom doorway. *It's fine. Maybe he's not here.*

I mustered my courage to look to my left. Tightening every muscle to brace myself, I took a look. It was clear there as well. I inhaled deeply to calm my shot nerves. And moved my gaze to the foot of the bed.

My breath caught in my throat. He stood there. Black against the darkness. The looming shape of a man. Horrific in its lack of detail. It wasn't human. It advanced to my side of the bed. *What does it want from me?* I thought of Stephen King's novels. The evil. The violence. The devil. I couldn't move. Even if I did move, I couldn't escape it.

A scream bounced against the walls. I sounded like I'd been attacked, even though he'd never touched me.

He dissolved into the moonless night.

The hall light snapped on. "What's the matter? Are you okay? Ken raced into the room, running past the point where the shadow person had stood.

"I saw him again."

"Again?" his voice sleepy, bewildered.

My heart pounds. "I'm sorry. I didn't mean to wake you."

He walked over, sat on the bed and hugged me. "It's just a dream. You know, I'd never let anything happen to you. Try to go back to sleep." He kissed me, then stood.

"It wasn't a dream. I was awake," I said, even though I knew what he'd reply.

"You were probably sleeping so lightly you thought you were awake. It was a nightmare."

I grabbed his hand. I didn't want to be alone. I suppressed the urge to ask him to stay; he had to be up in just three hours.

His lips brushed my forehead. "It's okay. Really. See you in the morning."

Reluctantly, I released his hand.

He shut off the hall light and shuffled back to his room. He stirred for a moment, then nothing. My sightings had become so frequent—a couple times a week for almost two months now—he'd fall easily asleep afterward.

I turned on my lamp and listened for sirens or my neighbors' voices. Any indication my scream had wakened them and they worried about my welfare. Nothing. Either they'd slept through my trauma or they just didn't care.

I propped myself up in bed. I craved a normal couple's restful night. Of cuddling next to the one I love in a peaceful, safe slumber. Just another normal activity disease had taken away from me. If Ken had been in the same bedroom as me, I would wake with each turn of his body, every soft sporadic snore. My sleep was too fragmented already. With Ken beside me, I'd feel much safer, but I'd never get any shuteye. I couldn't sacrifice the little sleep I'd get for the comfort of having him there beside me.

I finished my bedside glass of water and got up to refill it. I passed by the photos of my grandparents, and wondered if they ever had to contend with something like this. When I returned, I slid my Bible out from the nightstand drawer and embraced the leather-bound book. As I did after each sighting, I prayed for God to keep this apparition away from me. *Why isn't my Lord helping me?*

I didn't need this. My health had been spiraling downward. At the most, I slept four hours a night, and not straight through—more like 30 to 40 minutes at a time before thirst, pain or a noise awoke me. Comfort was elusive. No matter how deep a relaxed state I achieved, I just lay there wishing for the night to pass more quickly.

I had to sleep. I needed to function at work. I wanted to hang on to enough energy to do something besides work. I wanted a life. And work wasn't it.

I flipped off the light, closed my eyes and pressed my Bible against my chest.

Could I have opened some psychic sense after discussing the Circus Master with my Mom? I wondered if the shadow man had been there all along, and I just couldn't see him before. I guess it didn't matter. I needed to get rid of him. The condo felt differently than it once had. It had stopped being my haven.

I didn't want to tell Janice. It would just encourage her, when all I wanted was to squelch those so-called talents. Nightly, I pleaded to God to stop all this. To help me follow divine will. I didn't want all this psychic nonsense. Why did it keep pursuing me?

If this was some cosmic joke, I wasn't laughing.

~8~
The Sensitive

I sat at the check-in desk for the second annual ghost conference. Fifty-six people have enrolled, a group that crossed all races, genders and ages. The teen Goth cloaked in black. The 75-year-old Catholic who donned a crucifix. A Native American couple who held hands. A diverse group with invisible connections: grieving the loss of a loved one or seeking answers to an unsettling paranormal experience.

Last year, I'd looked on as an outsider, but this time I was as bound to them as they were to me. I joined with them in hopes of finding answers to our personal dilemmas.

My diseased body rebelled—having been robbed of its Saturday laziness to get up early for work. My hardened, atrophied muscles felt bloated, bulging against my skin; my joints screamed out with every movement, each gesture; and even my skin burned just from touching the silkiness of my blouse. I couldn't remember how it felt to live without constant pain. And my mind operated as if mired in a maze—navigating pathways of fuzz. I craved my bed.

The conference was about to begin and I signed-in the last person on my list. A cowboy—lanky with a handlebar mustache—stood in front of me, but wouldn't meet my gaze. "I'm lookin' forward to hearin' the stories. Figure a person doesn't get to do this every day." He adjusted his silver belt buckle. "Personally, I don't believe in all this ghost stuff. I thought it'd be interestin'. You know, hearin' what other people think."

Hardly anyone admitted they believed in the paranormal when they first arrived. It wasn't until they felt safe and knew they wouldn't be judged that they confessed the true reason they attended. *We are all so fragile; so afraid of being judged and not accepted.*

I handed the cowboy his packet and said, "Well, you'll certainly hear some very interesting stories today."

"Hope so," he said as he ambled into the lecture hall.

I boxed up the registration materials, slid them under the table and joined the conference in progress. I stood just inside the door in case I'd be needed.

Jason—who referred to himself as a sensitive, one who senses spirits but doesn't communicate with them—spoke to the audience with a large white board behind him. "It was then I learned I had a gift, one passed down the generations in my family. That's why my grandmother wasn't surprised when I saw her mother's spirit."

Being psychic is genetic? Brown hair. Dimples. ESP. I thought of my mother and wondered if anything else had happened to her.

Jason continued. "As a Hawaiian, I grew up with a strong oral tradition. My family shared and preserved its ghost stories. It's a very natural thing for us to do. People ask me if they can be a sensitive. Yes. You can. I believe everyone has the ability, but it's our different cultural and religious backgrounds that dictate whether our abilities are nurtured or suppressed." His brunette hair, longer than the too-short-cropped-look that was in fashion, bounced a little with each turn of his head.

A college-aged girl raised her hand.

Jason nodded to her.

"Your bio says you have a degree in comparative religions. So how do you reconcile your experiences with your religious beliefs? Does it affirm your belief in God or do you believe in God at all?"

I stepped away from the door, trying to escape the noise in the hall.

"Good question. I'm Jewish and I've found my abilities have drawn me closer to God. My experiences reinforce my beliefs in a higher power. Because I've embraced my sensitivity, I possess a greater sense of spirituality and peace. Any other questions?"

I considered his answer and wondered if the same could be possible for me. To use the odd experiences of late to forge a closer relationship with God. I shook my head. If anything, all this weirdness distanced me from The Great I Am. I couldn't reconcile why the Lord would allow all this evilness to haunt me if the divine truly loved me.

My religious beliefs weren't what they were when I first became a Born-Again Christian. My views had evolved, broadened. Even though Jesus sang to my heart and I valued my personal relationship with my savior, I'd come to believe the Lord had built many avenues for people to get to know him. Why would the Almighty have created so many different cultures with One-Religion-Fits-All? Through civilized debates with Muslims, Hindus and Jews, I'd found we shared many similarities in our religious tenets: love, respect, helping others and more. It was clear to me that each faith came with a different messenger to deliver very similar ideas.

But while my mind had opened regarding other religions, I hadn't reconciled how my paranormal experiences could bring me closer to God. I read my nightly Bible chapter and prayed daily, but I was scared. Frightened of the strange path my life was on. Terrified that I'd traveled down the wrong fork in the road. Could the Great I Am have told me to turn right, but perhaps in my stubborn mindset, I'd veered to the left?

The audience clapped. Participants rushed to Jason, who was swallowed by people hungry for information. Rapid-fire words competed in the acoustically perfected room. I could no longer see him. I'd never get one-on-one time with him. I sighed.

I walked down toward the mass encircling Jason and sat nearby, hoping the crowd dispersed soon enough for me to talk to him and find out how I could stop the shadow person from visiting me.

The cowboy came over. "This is great. I'm so glad I came," he said. "You know, I had something strange happen to me, but no one's ever believed me. Can I tell you about it?"

"Of course." I scooted over to the next seat so he could sit down. I smelled a hint of cologne.

"I used to live in an old house. Near Winnemucca." He looked right at me with tired brown eyes.

I worked to focus on him, on his conversation. My concentration was shot. My eyes caught the gleam of his shirt's pearl snaps. How they shined in those fluorescent lights. *Focus.* He needed to talk and I wanted to be receptive. I nodded.

"This sounds strange. A man still lived there; he died before I ever moved in. The smell of tobacco—I don't smoke myself—would appear out of nowhere. The stench almost overwhelmin'. Then the drawers, they'd open, then close by themselves. But that wasn't the worst thing."

He wrung the handouts into a twisted tube. "One day while I shaved, this man with a long gray beard stared at me in the mirror. I yelled and dropped my razor. It fell on the floor, but I didn't care. I turned around. He was gone. I thought someone broke in—that's how real he looked. I ran through the house, but everything was locked. I was alone. I told my friends. They laughed as if I was tellin' a joke. Later, they started worrin' about me. Sayin' I was alone too much and it was all in my head. Well, I know my mind and I never made anything up."

"I believe you," I said. The earnestness of his face, his tentative brown eyes, the way he clenched his hands showed his need to unburden himself. "How frightening. I can't imagine seeing a ghost look back at me from a mirror."

His whole countenance relaxed and a slight smile lifted his face. "Thank you. I can't tell you how many years I wanted to tell someone and have them believe me. Have them not think I'm some psycho. Thanks again."

He shook my hand vigorously. "Guess I better stretch my legs a bit before the next speaker."

I didn't want to suppress my fears for years. To have them fester like they did with the cowboy. Nor did I want to see someone stare back at me in the mirror. I must stop all this nonsense in my life before it escalated.

The group around Jason thinned to one elderly lady. I overheard her thanking him and I jumped up to claim my place. I checked my watch. I had three minutes until the next session started.

The gray-haired woman looked at me. "He's very good," she said. "Very good."

"Thanks," he said, almost shyly.

The woman walked off.

"Jason, great job. I...uh...I have a personal question for you. Something's been happening to me and I really need a couple minutes of your time."

"Of course."

I lowered my voice, since the room's acoustics were pin-drop good and the last thing I wanted was for my boss to hear my concerns. "I keep seeing a shadow person in my home. He appears by my bed or sometimes stands in the doorway." I took a deep breath. I guess I needed to purge myself. "I'm terrified. I think he's evil. I can't sleep afterward because I'm so frightened. What can I do?"

He nodded a bit. "Why are you so scared?"

"I don't know what he wants. But it's the fear—the absolute horror—rooted deep inside of me. It's, it's awful."

A person came up behind me. Jason spoke up. "I'm sorry, but we're discussing conference business. Would you mind giving us a few moments? I can meet you out in the hall when I'm done."

The steps retreated.

"Thank you," I said.

"Has anything happened at your house lately? Something that might make a spirit start appearing? Has anyone you known died recently? Do you play with Ouija boards?"

"No. None of that."

"How long have you lived there? What about the house's history?" He spoke quickly.

"About 15 years. The condo was new when I moved in. No one except for me and my boyfriend have lived there." I glanced at my watch. I heard my boss talking to the next speaker. *Please don't come over.*

Jason lowered his voice. "Okay. This is what you need to do. Take control. There's no reason to be terrified. He's startling you because you don't understand why he's visiting you."

My boss and the next speaker walked by us. We nodded to them.

He continued. "The way I see it, you have two choices: either ask him what he wants from you or tell him he's not welcome to visit you."

I can boss spirits around? Taking control of the situation never had occurred to me. After all, in how many Hollywood movies had the victims told spirits to disappear and been obeyed? If they had, the spirits would've gotten even madder and eviler. I cocked my head to the side. "Won't he get angry? Won't that make it worse?"

He chuckled, but not in a condescending way. "No. It's your house. It's your body. You take control and he'll listen. This isn't a horror novel. There's a reason he's there."

"I don't know what that could be," I replied.

"Well, perhaps someone else in your building opened a portal between worlds, like playing with a Ouija board—people don't realize what they're messing with. It could be why he's appearing."

Janice approached the mike to announce the next speaker.

"But why am I seeing him?" I asked.

"Because Kathy, you are a sensitive."

"No. Really—"

Jason shook his head. "Look, nothing will get better until you face the reality of your abilities. You need to develop them. Take charge. The spirits will listen to you. When does he disappear?"

"When I scream."

Everyone took their seats. Jason and I headed to the exit.

"See. He leaves because he's frightened you. You need to take control." He winked at me with his brown, thickly lashed eyes. "You can do it. Don't worry; he'll respect your wishes."

"Thanks, so much Jason. I really appreciate it."

"Practice being open, being more aware. And when spirits materialize, speak to them."

That night, I entered a spiritual tailspin. *Why would God do this to me?* I'd tried to be a good Christian, a kind person. I'd read every word in the Bible. Seven times. I prayed every day. I'd always believed that psychics were from the dark side. How could I be developing these skills when I walked on the side of the Lord?

I needed to deal with this. I pleaded with God for my soul. To rescue me. To save me once again and give me a normal life. I curled up with my Bible and eventually fell asleep.

A week or so later, the shadow visited once again. All I heard was the hum of the clock radio. Slowly, I peeked over to my bedside. He was there. So close I could touch him, though I doubted I'd feel anything in his dark gauzy silhouette. Frozen, I replayed Jason's advice to me. I pushed down the horror. Pushed it down to and through the soles of my feet. *Take control. I can do this.* I whispered, "Please leave. You are not welcome here. I need to sleep."

The shadow dissolved. I stared at the blank, dark wall. *I did it! He actually obeyed me!*

I sat up in bed. I wanted to wake Ken. To have him share in my victory. To say I stood up against something that terrified me. Then the realization hit me. I lay back down. I couldn't tell Ken. He believed they'd been nightmares. He wouldn't understand.

I thought of the cowboy. "Then they started worryin' about me."

So I kept my victory to myself.

My body melted into the mattress. I thanked God, then I mentally thanked Jason. The shadow person was gone. And he stayed away. At least for awhile.

~9~

Psychic Development

More than a year passed with no appearance by the shadow man. A blissfully quiet period of normalcy. Perhaps, God had answered my prayers. Or, maybe, I'd passed the Lord's test.

Anastasia, the new manager in charge of the ghost conference, sat at my conference table. I'd moved up in the world of offices. No longer did I work in a windowless storage area, sharing my space with Biff the Mannequin. Now my office, located on the top floor, commanded a sweeping Sierra view.

We were meeting to review the ghost conference participant evaluations. This was the first year I hadn't been involved in any of the planning. I hadn't even attended the lectures.

"Overall, the feedback's great," Anastasia said with her lilting voice that combined a soft Mexican accent with clear, well-spoken English.

"People liked the lectures, but they missed not having any ghost investigations," she said. "You know it's interesting. I don't believe in all this stuff, but I can see why people come. It seemed cathartic for them."

I nodded as I scanned the goldenrod summary sheets. My finger stopped at the question of what they'd like to see in the future. "Wow. Have you gotten down to what they want to see next year? It's almost unanimous. They want the psychic you brought in to teach again. Look," I pointed out the long paragraph. "Almost every entry mentions her."

The typed list was a veritable Vickie Gay love fest.

"Have Vickie teach us how to become psychic."

"Vickie was fascinating. I want to learn more about her abilities."

"She's the real thing. I've never met a real psychic before. Thank you!"

"The psychic gave the best presentation ever. I want to hear more."

"I want to learn how to talk to my relatives who've passed over."

"Bring Vickie back, have her speak longer."

Vickie, Vickie, Vickie in just about every suggestion.

"Yes. While she was at the conference, there were always people waiting to ask her questions." Anastasia pushed her straight brown hair away from her face. "We'll have to bring her back."

An idea occurred to me. "We used to offer ghost-type classes. They did really well. You should put some up again…late spring or early summer, so they won't compete with the conference, but could help us build our event mailing list. Janice would teach again, I'm sure. And if you could get Vickie to teach people how to develop their psychic abilities—that could be big!"

"I love it." She glanced at her watch. "I better get going." Anastasia stood up and paused at the doorway. "You know, maybe we can take it and then we'll just offer standing-room only classes!"

We laughed.

My phone rang.

"Go ahead and get it. I'll let you know what Vickie says," Anastasia said as she turned and headed back to her office at the end of the hall.

I picked up the receiver. "Hello, TMCC Workforce Development and Continuing Education. I'm Kathy. How can I help you?"

I heard someone fidget. Probably a wrong number.

I was about to speak again when a woman began talking. "I know this sounds strange, but I was told I needed to call this number. Did you say this is Truckee Meadows Community College?"

"Yes, it is. I'm Kathy, the marketing manager for the college's noncredit programs. How can I help you?"

"I'm not sure." She paused as if she was confused. "I'm Vickie Gay. I spoke at the TMCC conference. Last month."

What a coincidence. "Yes, Vickie. You and I spoke briefly in September regarding a press release my intern wrote." She probably wanted a copy of the newspaper article, which featured her.

"Oh, right. I'm sorry, I didn't remember." Her voice was pleasant, yet professional. "That was a nice article in the newspaper."

"Would you like me to send you a copy?"

"No. Thank you. I called about something else."

I was puzzled why she'd phone me. "Okay."

"This is going to sound strange. While meditating, I was told to call your number because you had news for me."

"Really? Who would say that?"

"My spirit guide."

A chill reverberated through my body. *She was told I had news for her?* There was no way for her to know. Anastasia had been in the doorway when the phone rang, so I know she didn't talk to her. "Why call me? Why not Anastasia?"

"He gave me your number. He said you'd have news for me. Do you?"

Does she know we were talking about her? I was taken aback. I glanced at the pine tree next to my window. A raven hopped around the branch closest to the pane. I took a breath to compose myself and thought back to our brief phone conversation in September. There wasn't a reason to give her my number, as we had taken care of everything right then. "It's funny you happened to call right now. Anastasia just left my office. And we did talk about you." I spoke a little too fast.

"Yes."

Calm down. The raven, shiny black, leaned toward the glass as if he was peering at me. "Everyone at the conference raved about you. In fact, Anastasia's getting ready to call you to see if you'd like to teach a class for us. She couldn't have left my office more than a minute ago."

"That must be what I tapped into," Vickie said with conviction.

"She wants you to teach this summer."

"Mmmm, interesting," she said. "I travel a great deal, so I need to check my calendar."

"Well, Anastasia's the one setting it up. I'm sure she'll call you soon." I wondered if Vickie was eavesdropping on my own mind at that very moment. Uncovering all my secrets. I felt exposed, naked.

"Sounds good. I'd like to teach for the college. Thank you, Kathy."

"Thank you. It was nice speaking with you."

I hung up. The raven hopped to another branch, paused, then flew off.

She's the real deal. But, it seemed so preposterous. So out there. But how could she have known, otherwise? No one else had been around. I ran out of my office to tell Anastasia.

TMCC's Develop Your Psychic Abilities class was scheduled for July. Vickie and her talent intrigued me. Even after mulling over my conversation with her, I couldn't find a logical reason for how she would've known to call. I fixated on this course. About signing up to find out if I was really psychic.

Don't get me wrong. I liked having my normal life back. It was just I wasn't sure it would stay that way. I woke up four or five times every night with this disease. Four or five times I was afraid to look around. When I got up for a drink of water or to use the bathroom, I put on self-imposed blinders; I fixed my eyes to the carpet. The fear that a shadow person could appear was too strong. Even after a year.

I decided to pray on it. Each night, I asked for guidance on whether or not I should take that class. I prayed for God's will to be done. Night after night, no answer. The class started to fill.

Ken's mother (although Ken and I weren't married, I considered her my mother-in-law) phoned me to see if I wanted to go to Vickie's class with her, as I had told her about my encounter with Vickie. My mouth engaged before my brain kicked in, "I'd love to. I'll sign us up tomorrow." I hung up, put my head in my hands and hoped I'd made the right choice.

I registered us online, foregoing my employee discount. I didn't want my coworkers to know I was taking this class. Colleges could be judgmental places and I didn't want to place myself at the podium for ridicule. Normal, educated and rational people didn't take up ESP.

Even when I hadn't believed in psychics or the paranormal, I still defended the right of holding these classes when others at the college condemned them. Professors complained, saying we shouldn't legitimize such silliness. So, the administration required us to include a disclaimer wherever we mentioned ghost/psychic/paranormal classes that the school did not endorse these subjects or the content taught.

So, why did I defend these classes? It was because we are a community-based department of the college, funded by the students who enrolled in our noncredit programs. If there was enough interest to cover class expenses, what right did we have to judge the topic or the people taking the course? What about the freedom of speech and the sharing of ideas academia was supposed to promote?

Some ideals reached beyond higher education's openness. Due to my support of these classes, the college grapevine had carried the message I'd gone all ghosty. And my coworkers didn't know about my paranormal experiences. If they had, some would have stopped talking to me entirely.

So I manufactured reasons why I was taking Vickie's class.

"I'm just curious." *No. Won't work.*

"After seeing the teacher's conference evaluations, I wanted to see what the hoopla's about." *No. That implies I'm interested in this stuff.*

"My mother-in-law really wanted to take it, but she didn't want to go alone. So I told her I'd accompany her." *Possibly. I'm just being a good daughter-in-law and providing companionship.*

Someone at work would find out. Whoever pulled the class roster would see my name at the top of the list. Berry, Kathleen.

What a louse I was for using Anne as a virtual human shield. But I justified it, as I knew we'd have a good time. And I'd grown excited about taking the class.

The course sold out, generating a lengthy waiting list. Anne and I arrived early for the first class to stake out our seats. It was a typical classroom at the TMCC Meadowood Center. A wall of windows framed the landscaped pines outside. A white board ran the length of the room. Vickie was already there, and her appearance stopped me dead. She was beautiful. Taller than me, probably around 5'10''. Trim—she must've worked out. Long, thick, golden tresses reached the small of her back. She wore black slacks and a peasant blouse. I guessed she wasn't much older than me.

Anne sat. I went to introduce myself.

"Hi, I'm Kathy. I'm the marketing person for WDCE. We've talked on the phone."

"Yes. It's good to meet you." She shook my hand. Her face radiated peacefulness, an unconditional acceptance of life.

"You've got a full class," I told her.

"Wonderful!" she said. "Do you have the roster?"

A voice rang out from the back of the class. "I've got it." It was Marni *(not her real name)*, my coworker. She stood up from a desk that had her purse, a notebook and a pen on it. She walked up to us giggling under her breath.

Crap! No one had asked me about this class, so I figured God had showed me grace by not having them notice my name. The room suddenly felt sweltering.

Marni, smiling like a Cheshire cat, handed Vickie the roster and looked at me a bit sideways. "You didn't tell me you were taking this class. I saw your name on the roster today. I thought I was the only one at work who would take it," she said.

"I'm here with my mother-in-law. Anne." Guiltily, I pointed to the distinguished older woman with cropped, curly red hair and large, framed glasses. "Anne, this is Marni, who works in my office. And Marni, Vickie, this is my mother-in-law, Anne."

Anne smiled. "Nice to meet you both."

I needed to watch what I would say and do. I couldn't have everyone thinking I'd gone weird. At least odder than they'd already thought I was. Why was Marni taking this class? Perhaps things had happened to her too? For a split second, I pondered asking her why. But just as quickly, I dismissed the idea. I couldn't risk reciprocation. I returned to my seat.

"All right. Let's get started," Vickie said. She explained her goals for the class, then asked each of us to share why we wanted to develop our psychic abilities.

What the hell am I going to say? I certainly couldn't tell the truth with Marni here.

One woman spoke up, "I'm taking this class because I think I have a psychic ability with animals."

"Ahh, good," Vickie said. "Some people have very clear connections with animals."

My mind raced for a safe response to the question. My palms sweated. I couldn't quite make myself fess up that I'd seen shadow people. Not now.

"Kathy? It's your turn," Vickie said.

I looked opposite Marni's direction. "Hi, I'm Kathy, I work here at TMCC and I'm here, because I'm just...curious. There have been, um, coincidences in my life." My voice shook.

Anne grinned at me in understanding.

"There are no coincidences, Kathy," Vickie stated. "There's a reason for everything. A purpose to why you took this class. Even a reason why you're sitting next to the people you are. You may not know it now, but there is one." Vickie said this with conviction, like there was no room for argument.

No coincidences? A bit overreaching, isn't it?

Of course, I knew why I was taking this class. At least, I think I did. I'm so absorbed by this concept that I missed Marni's reason for being there.

An older, balding man exclaimed, "I don't believe any of this. I just wanted to see what you had to say."

"Well, I appreciate you being open-minded enough to join us," Vickie said, then turned to the rest of the class. "Here are some basic beliefs I have in regard to psychic abilities and mediumship. First, never pry into someone's thoughts. It's an invasion of privacy and not a legitimate reason to develop your abilities. I must admit, there've been times with my teenage daughter when I'd like to find out what she's thinking, but I don't."

The class laughed.

"And if I can avoid the temptation, then everyone else can too. I reserve this skill for when someone asks me to tap in.

"Now, let's discuss the difference between psychics and mediums. Everyone is psychic. We're all born with the ability to pick up on the thoughts of the collective. Even objects can carry psychic details about us. That's called psychometry. Later, you'll learn how to read someone's personal possessions to pick up on their feelings and messages.

"All mediums are psychic. Mediums directly communicate with spirits, guides and those who have crossed over. Not everyone is a medium."

I scribbled notes on my yellow legal pad. She presented this far-out information so matter-of-factly, I'd started to accept these notions may have validity. I remembered seeing her resume come across my desk. A former accountant. College graduate. Small business owner.

"Okay. It's time for your first exercise. I want you to practice this each day. Even if you can only do it for five minutes, it'll help you on your quest to build your senses. First, we'll say a prayer for protection and place a white light around us. Then we'll ask spirit to come visit us. Don't worry. I'll be watching out for you."

Say a prayer. I like that. If God is involved, this can't be evil, right?

"Close your eyes and uncross your arms and legs. Crossing your body parts blocks energy and you need to be open to be successful. Place your feet flat on the ground."

Interesting. Eastern medicine believed the same thing. When I went to Japanese Restoration Therapy, my therapist told me to uncross my arms so the flow of energy wasn't obstructed.

I opened my arms and placed my hands palm up on a desk where students figured out math problems and took history tests.

"Let's visualize a room. A comfortable room. One you can decorate in any way you want to make it yours. Then, place a chair across from you for spirit to sit in."

I conjured a room in a Victorian mansion, one with narrow, bay-like windows in the corner of the room. A sun-filled space. I decorated it with Ken's wildlife portraits, my Aunt Ruby's quilts, my grandmother's watercolors, family photos, flowers and lace curtains. The colors were soft, relaxing—powder pinks, rose, winter white and blues. My open seat was an antique tapestry chair, the kind with an oval back.

Vickie continued. "Say this with me: I call upon the highest, most positive spirit to come through now!"

I heard the students murmuring as I braced myself for a spirit visitor.

"Picture spirit coming through the door, then sitting in the chair you've placed before you…Talk to him or her."

The room went quiet. Nothing was in my head or in my invented room. I called for the highest and most positive once again. No feelings. Nada. Nothing came through. I was alone. *Why didn't anything happen?*

I sat there quietly. Time moved slowly. I went through the exercise again in my head, willing something, anything to happen. I opened one eye and glanced about the room. Everyone sat calmly. No one else peeked, so I quickly shut it again before I was discovered.

"Please thank spirit for visiting and then tell it good-bye."

She waited a moment. "Open your eyes."

Everyone looked at each other. Few faces appeared triumphant.

"Who made contact?"

My mother-in-law shook her head no.

A few hands rose.

"I had something in my chair, but I didn't get any message from it," a middle-aged bleached blonde said.

"I felt a tingling. But nothing else," stated a woman who was probably a flower child of the sixties.

"All good starts," Vickie commented.

The balding man –the one who didn't believe in any of this—raised his hand. "I had a conversation with my father. Quite a lengthy one. It was amazing. He told me things he'd never told me before." His eyes dart around the room, avoiding eye contact with Vickie.

"Really? Have you done this before?" she asked.

"No. But it all happened. It was wonderful. I'm psychic!"

I didn't believe him. No one else had gotten much and there's this guy coming up with fantastic stories.

Vickie stayed placid, unflappable. "Well that's very good, isn't it?" she said pleasantly, but without enthusiasm. Addressing the rest of the class, she said, "Don't be discouraged if nothing happens. It takes practice to get good results. Meditate with an open mind and release your fears. To do this, you must realize spirits are just people without bodies. The soul lives on; it is energy. Talk to a physicist and he'll tell you energy doesn't disappear. So when your body dies, your energy—your soul—survives.

"Also, you don't invite every stranger to your home. In the same way, be picky about the spirits you connect with. That's why you only ask for the highest and best to come through."

I nodded. Yet, this was all so weird, like a *Twilight Zone* episode. But at the same time, my heart and my brain wanted to experience more than what I could normally see or hear. As long as it didn't frighten me or alienate me from God.

Vickie wasn't what I expected from a psychic. She wasn't flighty or spooky. And she didn't come across as Satanic. While I still believed many con artists labeled themselves psychic, I no longer believed that all psychics were hucksters.

I shook my head as my thoughts sunk in. Why did I keep applying negative stereotypes? So far, none of the paranormal folks I'd met had fit those expectations. Prior to exploring the paranormal, they had been engineers, mathematicians, managers, accountants and even a physicist.

Hardly dim-witted people. Many encouraged skepticism and didn't mind being challenged. My mind went to Janice. She was in gaming management prior to becoming a ghost researcher. She was smart, rational and had an open mind—like most of the paranormal experts I'd met.

Layers of negativity unraveled. How ironic that I'd judged these people when I experienced odd circumstances myself. I'd kept closing myself off to any possibility of possessing a sixth sense, so I would not be like *them*.

I meditated every weekday morning before I left for work. Nothing happened. At each subsequent class, more students reported their skills improving. I was a complete failure. Nothing came through. I wasn't even getting fifty percent right on the classroom exercises. I performed worse than the odds!

Jason and Janice had to be wrong. I was not a sensitive. I wasn't even average. A lot of the people in the class were having breakthroughs. I wasn't. Perhaps Vickie's wrong. Not everyone could be psychic.

It surprised me this thought didn't make me happy.

~10~
There Are No Coincidences

On a hot cloudless July day, I stared out the window waiting for my work email to load.

I scanned the inbox. *Faculty debating the true freedom of speech.* Delete. *Needed: A Computer Printer.* Delete. *Media Request.* I opened an e-mail from our college's public information office informing me that a local TV anchor wanted us to arrange a ghost hunt for the news. *How odd.* These requests normally didn't pop up until mid-October. I flipped through my Rolodex, dialed his number. It rang three times.

"Bill Brown here."

"Hi Bill. This is Kathy Berry from TMCC. I understand you want to go on a ghost hunt?"

"Yes. Can you set it up?" A police scanner squawked in the background.

"Of course. The speakers are set up for the next conference. I can arrange for them to meet you somewhere."

"Great. I want to do something a little different: an in-depth series on ghost hunting. To have my crew spend the night with your experts in several haunted locations to see if there's anything to all this ghost hunting business."

"You want to spend the night?" Normally, reporters spent a couple hours at a location, just enough time to get footage for a two- to three-minute segment they'd air on Halloween.

"Yeah. I want to put in the time and resources to do it right. That's why I want to start on it now. Can you help me?"

"Of course."

"Can you set up a meeting next Thursday at 10 a.m. at Walden's Coffee?"

"I'll try. I'll e-mail you and let you know if they're available." I hung up and laughed. A group spending the night in a haunted location! Better them than me!

I arrived ten minutes early to talk with the conference speakers before we met Bill. Janice was there, as well as Ted and Cheryl *(not their real identities)*—siblings who specialize in electronic voice phenomena. I'd never met them, but Anastasia assured me they'd be great.

The coffee house was packed for 10 a.m. on a workday. The noise of thirty different conversations bounced off the walls. I walked into the bustling little restaurant to see Janice with two other people in the corner.

My gaze fell on Cheryl. This buxom woman sported thick, wavy, brown locks that must've reached mid-way down her back. She wore an embroidered peasant blouse as well as a look of serenity. When I got close to the table, I noticed her fuchsia fingernails reaching at least a good half-inch from her fingertips.

Next to Cheryl, Ted sat without a hint of emotion on his face. Soft coiled curls, hugged his scalp, just covering his ears. He wore camouflage pants and a t-shirt over his wiry frame.

Janice pushed out the chair next to her with her foot. "Good to see you. This is Cheryl and Ted."

"Nice to meet you." I shook their hands before dropping into the seat.

"Thanks so much for including us, Kathy," Cheryl said in a soft voice tinged with a faded New York accent. "We've never been on TV. Oh, what fun this'll be!" Her large, green eyes shone with excitement.

I love her enthusiasm.

My role at this meeting was to provide logistical support to further the story and ensure the ghost conference received publicity. Then once I'd accomplished this, I'd bow out and wait for the story to air. Some thought that because I worked in public relations I sought the spotlight, but it was quite the opposite. I felt most comfortable in the wings as a support person.

Bill Brown, a local broadcasting legend, strolled in. Wearing jeans and a T-shirt, he looked different from the suit-clad journalist I'd seen on TV. Yet, his trademark blonde hair and blue eyes remained the same.

I stood up and walked over to him. "Hi, I'm Kathy from TMCC."

He smiled broadly and shook my hand. "Thanks for arranging this. We're very excited at the station."

"I think you're going to enjoy doing these stories. Let's go meet your ghost hunters," I said as I led him through the tight pathway around tables and chairs.

After introductions, we discussed business.

Bill told us about his plans. "I know it seems too early to think about Halloween, but I want to do these stories right. And KTVN supports my vision. We'll have the investigative team spend the night in three haunted locations. We'll really take the time to explore the possibilities the paranormal may exist. No theatrics. No drama. Just journalism. If something happens, great. If we get nothing, it shows we found no proof of a haunting." He sips a cup of regular coffee.

"I love this," Janice said.

"Where shall we go?" Cheryl asked.

"You're the experts. Where should we go?" Bill replied.

An espresso machine sounded off, and my brain blanks out. *I hate this disease.* It took me a moment to re-focus on our group's conversation.

"Thunderbird Lodge near Lake Tahoe," Janice said.

"El Borracho Restaurant. We've heard stories," Cheryl said.

"Gold Canyon Steakhouse in Dayton," Janice said.

"All over Virginia City," said Ted.

I scribbled the locations on my yellow legal pad.

"Okay...good ideas. Perhaps we can go to places people may not think about. I'd like to do this big. Virginia City's been done a lot. What have other stations covered?"

"Most of the ones we mentioned, except for El Borracho," I said.

"If you want to do big, I have an idea," Janice suggested. "Are you interested in traveling out of the area?"

"Well, I'd like to stay in our viewing community—which covers most of the northern half of the state and some of the eastern Sierra. What did you have in mind?"

I leaned in closer to Janice, as there were too many distractions for my weary mind to follow the conversation well.

She replied, "I know the caretaker of the Goldfield Hotel. You know, in central Nevada. They don't usually let people inside. It's been closed for decades. But there's a chance I could get us in. It'd have to be a small group, but I can contact her if you'd be interested."

"Hmmm. It's a bit out of the way, but, yes. Please look into it."

"Then, of course there's the Cal Neva Lodge up at Crystal Bay," Janice added. "It's haunted by Frank Sinatra and Marilyn Monroe."

"Sounds good," Bill said as he jotted notes in his small reporters' flip pad.

"If we did go to Goldfield, we could investigate the Tonopah World War II airbase as well," said Ted.

"If we do it, let's spend the night in the Mizpah! There's a ghost there that loves red shoes!" Janice clapped with excitement.

"How about the Levy Mansion?" Cheryl asks.

"There's always the Lake Mansion. I worked there for two years," I interjected, trying to contribute.

Bill frowned slightly. "Yeah, that's a great place, but they have a lot of kids' arts programs there. I'd hate to do anything to frighten children."

What a nice guy. "Oh. Of course, you're right. I didn't think of that." I sipped my chai latte.

"No problem. We've got a good list to pick from. Can you start making contact with the owners of these places to see who's interested? Then, we can proceed from there."

Cheryl, Ted, Janice and I divvied up the locations according to our personal contacts.

"Kathy, please coordinate and let me know where we stand in about a week," he said. "We should schedule our first night the middle of September. "I need to get budget approval from the station, especially if we head out of town."

"Will do." I slipped my ballpoint into my purse.

We stood and walked to the door. Janice stayed back, so I waited for her.

"You should come on the investigations with us," she said.

"You're always thinking of me." I gave her a hug.

"You could get a lot out of this."

The last thing I want to do is to spend the night in a "haunted" building. "My role's just to coordinate and get out of the way. There's nothing I can contribute to Bill's stories. You'll be okay on your own."

"Of course I will. I've done a ton of them. But you should think about it....How's your class with Vickie coming?"

"I'm glad I'm taking it—it's really fascinating—but I don't think I'm in the least bit psychic. I keep practicing and nothing's happening."

Janice smiled. "Perhaps you're trying too hard." We stopped at her sedan. "I've got to run, but promise me you'll think about coming? It'd be great if you did."

I'm not going to consider it, but I never want to disappoint Janice. "Okay."

The day before our last psychic class, Janice phoned. She'd arranged for KTVN and the investigators to spend the night in central Nevada's Goldfield Hotel. This was a coup, as the long-shuttered building rarely opened to the public. Once again, she encouraged me to go. I told her reporters didn't like to have PR people milling around. As soon as I hung up with Janice, I immediately emailed Bill the news.

The next morning, I read his response.

"Hi, Kathy,

Great news! After I received your message, I stayed up half the night researching the Goldfield Hotel. You can't imagine the stories I've found. Apparently, it's ranked among the most haunted sites in the country, so if nothing happens, it'll still make a good story. This is more than I hoped for. Call me.

Bill"

I phoned him at the newsroom. "Are you ready to get scared?"

Bill laughed boisterously.

I smiled at the contagiousness of his laughter.

"I hope so! I can't tell you how excited everyone is. Let's discuss logistics. We should carpool—maybe take two or even three vehicles with all the gear we'll need. Can someone in your group drive?"

"I'm sure someone can." I scribbled a note in my file to check on that.

"Is there a motel in town? We'll probably need a room or two so we have a place to go with running water. It'll be a long night, you know." He sounded like a child on Christmas Eve.

"I'll look into it. It's been a long time since I've been through Goldfield. You know, you guys will have a great experience, even if it's just to get inside a great old building."

Bill didn't immediately respond. I heard reporters chatter in the background. And a phone ring, before he spoke, "You're coming, aren't you?"

What? He wants me to come? Surely, he's just being polite. "Thanks. But. Umm…Bill, I don't see the point. I don't know much about the paranormal. I can't do anything to further your story. I'd just be in the way."

"You really should join us. You've helped so much," he paused. "The team could use an impartial observer. You could do that. It's not fair for you to set up the logistics and not come. How often will you get a chance like this?" He sounded sincere.

But what if I don't want to? I composed myself before I spoke. "Well, I don't know…I'll have to clear it with my boss."

"Good. Let me know what he says. There's so much to do. We need to figure out what to bring and get everything set. It'll be here before we know it."

I hung up the receiver and gazed at the mountains, considering my options. The trip could be an opportunity to get to know Bill better, and by getting better acquainted, it could be easier to pitch future classes for publicity.

But I don't want to go. Why? I asked myself. Did I really believe ghosts would come out and scare us? That we'd hear chains clanging down the hallway? No. Honestly, I couldn't imagine anything happening. But then again, I loved the idea of getting into that grand old building. And I also didn't want to look like a scaredy cat.

I'd ask my Dean for approval. If he said no, I'd be let off the hook. And, Janice had said the hotel caretaker said our group had to stay under eight people. Perhaps that could be my out.

◆　◆　◆

During the last psychic class, we positioned our one-person desks into a circle. Anne didn't feel well, so she didn't attend. Neither did Marni.

"Tonight, we're going to conduct a group reading," Vickie said from outside the circle. "First, we'll go into our meditative state and then I'll select a person for us to focus on. Make sure you say everything that comes to mind, but don't over think it."

We took each other's hands, said our prayers and called forward only the most positive spirits.

"All right, let's read Lisa."

I concentrated. I was especially weak that night and just sitting upright took a great effort.

"There's a man next to you," the woman beside me said. "He's holding his chest."

"Good." Vickie replied. "Ask him what he wants Lisa to know."

She muttered softly, and then paused. "Sorry. I don't get anything else. Lisa, do you know someone who had a heart attack?"

"I can't think of anyone," Lisa said.

Nothing popped into my mind as most of the class contributed to the reading. I'd given up on the notion I was psychic. Yeah, things had happened to me. But nothing consistent or predictable.

After class let out, Vickie and I left the building together. The pleasant, warm night was alive with the chirping of crickets and the voices of students eager to get home.

"Something happened today and I'm not sure what to do," I said, clutching my spiral ring notebook against my chest.

"What's that?" Vickie asked as she fished keys from her purse.

"KTVN's doing a ghost hunt. They're staying the night in the Goldfield Hotel with some of our conference speakers."

"I've heard it's an active place," she remarked. "So what's the problem?"

"Bill Brown wants me to go with them and I don't want to."

She stopped walking and faced me. "You need to go."

I shook my head.

"You must. Don't you understand?" She grasped my hand. "Goldfield is *why* you took this class."

"No, it isn't. I didn't know about any of this until today, and I never dreamed KTVN would want me to go."

She smiled slightly and squeezed my hand briefly before releasing it. "Remember what I said to you in our first class? There are no coincidences. We make arrangements with others before we're born. There are lessons to learn and purposes to achieve. You took this class so you would be prepared for Goldfield."

Wow, what a concept. "But…You see…I'm not prepared. I don't feel any more psychic today than when I started your class. I'm not very good at this. I just don't think I can do it." I pushed my fingers further into the notebook's spiral binding.

"Just remember everything I've taught you and you'll be fine. You *are* ready for this."

"I—" I didn't know what to say. I trusted Vickie and her skills.

"Have confidence. Remember, you're always in control. Nothing can harm you unless you let it. Don't be afraid. And, always wrap yourself in protection. This is happening now for a reason. You are more ready than you know. Be excited. This'll be a great opportunity for you!"

"Okay," I reply glumly. We resumed walking to our cars.

Vickie stopped at her van. "Remember—there are no coincidences. Call me afterwards to let me know how it goes."

She drove off while I stood in the dark parking lot absorbing what she said.

What have I gotten myself into?

~11~
Preparing for Goldfield

Nothing went wrong. I was bound for Goldfield.

Sigh.

Tasks fell into place as easily as a kayak skimming through reflective waters. My boss had approved my travel. The group had stayed under the eight-person limit. The hotel caretaker had secured final approval from the owner. In three days, we were to leave and all the things I had expected— or more honestly, had hoped—to go wrong to give me a graceful out had easily jelled.

There are no coincidences.

Laying on the couch, I surveyed the little piles on the living room floor that made up my Goldfield provisions. A small ice chest. Coat. Flashlight. Pillow. It was Sunday, and I'd started packing that morning, since I wouldn't have the strength or energy to do it after work. There was nothing left in me. I was so weak, I could barely move.

"Why don't you call Bill tomorrow and tell him you're not feeling up to this," Ken said as he stepped over my sleeping bag. "Look at you. You're not well enough to go. You've been going downhill now, for what, two months? Is this ghost chase worth risking your health? You're back to spending all your non-work time in bed or lying on the couch. After Goldfield, you may not be well enough to keep working."

"It's more complicated than that." I shivered and pulled the nearby fleece blanket around me. Lately, my body couldn't hold any heat. It was 74 degrees in here, but it seemed like 34.

He shook his head and disappeared into the bedroom. He returned with a down comforter. He dropped it on me and sculpted it around my body. "Do you want a hot water bottle, too?"

"No. I think this'll be enough." I patted him on the leg. "Thanks."

He stood next to the couch, looking down. "Please stay home."

"I can't. I just feel like I have to go. If I get worse, I'll go to the motel. You know, I'm also doing this for my job." I yelped, the nerve pain slicing me like a knife from my toe to my hip. I hated this damned pain, which crept up on me when I tried to relax. I took a couple deep breaths to recover from the pain.

"For someone who doesn't want to go, you're sure fighting for it," Ken said with a trace of irritation as he left the room.

When I had first met Ken in college, he would've been all over the idea of a ghost hunt. But now that he'd earned both a geology degree and an MBA, he's been much more logical. Practical. Scientific. I knew deep down that wasn't the real reason he wanted me to stay home. My deteriorating health concerned him. For so many years, he'd sat helplessly watching me writhe in pain; pain sometimes so severe even a bed sheet's weight reduced me to tears. He knew as well as I did, what triggered a relapse. And I'd be doing all of those things in Goldfield: long periods of standing, stress, staying up late. He must have thought I was crazy. Perhaps he was right.

I dragged myself to bed. Maybe I would take a sleeping pill and maybe it would work longer than four hours this time.

I wrapped my blankets around me. How I wished I could fall asleep quickly—not after three or four hours of being in bed. I started one of my deep-breathing exercises, the one where I count back from 100. 99. 98.

My mind reeled with thoughts of Goldfield. 97. *Am I stupid for going?* 96. *I really can't imagine anything happening.* 95. *Vickie did say it was an active site.* 94. *Could the Devil be fooling me into thinking I should go? What if God is testing me? If so, I'm failing miserably.*

Crud. I'd lost count. Relaxation exercises were futile tonight.

Dear Lord please give me a sign. If I'm delving into the underworld or straying from Your flock—please guide me back.

Physical comfort eluded me as well. I tried laying on my stomach one minute, but with this disease, I bloated badly. But when I swung over to my side, my back ached. Eventually, I lodged a pillow between my knees and fell asleep.

Then the nightmare—one that's plagued me every night for the past two weeks—invaded the little peaceful slumber I could catch.

First, the loud, crashing, rhythmic beat. Pound. Pound. Pound.
I stand outside the massive building looking in.
All of a sudden, I'm inside the dark hotel. In a cavernous room. The windows shuttered. I don't have a flashlight and it's the blackest black in here. I can't even see my hand in front of my face. Pound. Pound. Pound.
Where's the rest of the team? What way should I go? I rifle through my backpack groping for a flashlight, lantern. Anything.
"Bill? Janice? Anyone? Help me! I can't find my way out."
Pound. Pound. Pound.
Evil surrounds me, tightening its circle until I can feel its fetid breath all around me. Almost crushing me. It's so crowded, except I can't see anyone. Then the voices start, the clamor of a boisterous crowd. The pounding softens, forming an accompanying beat with a ragtime piano. The gaiety is not for me, it's for the others I can't see. They're anticipating something that's about to happen. I turn frigid, shiver. The air around me grows heavy, making it harder to breathe. I'd run, but am paralyzed, unable to flee the evil. Then I hear, "You should have never come to Goldfield."

I forced myself awake then, unwilling to see what would happen next. I still heard the pounding. I panicked, before I realized the noise was my own heart beating.

I extricated myself from my blanket cocoon and stumbled into the bathroom. I propped my elbows on the sill of the opened window, the chill from the night air bracing me. The moon illuminated our backyard, the trees throwing long shadows. Was this dream a warning or just an irrational fear? What if it was a sign, a message from the Almighty to stay home? But all the "coincidences" had fallen into place. And, it felt like my life had been heading in this direction for a reason.

The form of a cottontail hopped along the newly placed topsoil.

"God, I don't know what to do. Please help me," I whispered. "If you do not want me to go to Goldfield, I won't. Just let me know."

I returned to bed and tried once again to get comfortable. *The Lord has always taken care of me. Why should I worry?* I thought of all the investigations Janice had gone on over the years. She told me she was never afraid. Nothing evil had happened to her. And, thanks to Vickie, I knew the prayer for protection. What was the worst that could happen?

I needed to get back to sleep. I tried a different relaxation exercise. *Inhale deeply. Tighten my feet. Exhale. Relax them. Breathe in. Make my ankles heavy. Lighten up. Tighten my calves. Loosen them....*

I kept up with the meditation I learned in Vickie's class, even though I'd never made any contact. I did it more for the few hours of increased energy it brought me—a great plus with my health teetering on the precipice. It also cleared my mind for a time. Thinking clearly was a luxury, one most healthy people wouldn't think to appreciate.

I decided to meditate in the backyard. As I slid open the glass door, a thin black beak dipped down from the rain gutter. Then a little blue and black face with white feathered eyebrows peered down at me.

"Hi, Gutter. Want a peanut?"

The scrub jay righted himself. I heard his steps prancing on the aluminum of the gutter.

"Okay. But these are your last." I held out two in-shell peanuts: one for Gutter and the other for his mate, Shy, who hid from me most of the time. I threw them out to the middle of the yard. Gutter swooped down on the nuts, picked one up, dropped it, picked up the other and then flew off squawking. Shy bobbed up and down in the ash tree, making a prolonged nag-like call, before she descended to get Gutter's discarded nut.

I walked to the granite boulder, next to the newly planted Vanderwolf Pine. I relaxed, prayed for protection and called in the highest and best to help me.

Whoa. What's that? I actually feel something! My hands tingled. I brought myself back into the meditation and tried to stay calm. I asked, "Is someone here?"

"Yes" popped into my brain and I realize it was my Great Aunt Ruby.

I started to question myself. It must have been my imagination. But even logically, I had a hard time believing it, having been so consumed by Goldfield that I hadn't thought about Ruby in some time. So why would my mind pull her up now if she hadn't been there?

"Is this really Ruby?"

Love enveloped my tired, weak body. I heard another faint "Yes."

Oh my God! I've made contact! I fumbled. I tried to remember how Vickie said we should handle contacts. I concentrated and focused my energies. "What have you come to show me?"

"You are on the right path."

My hands trembled and tears migrated down my cheeks. "Thank you." I was swept away in gratitude, love and sadness for the loss of my beloved aunt who had died several years ago. "I've missed you so much. I love you."

"I love you. You will be fine."

The tingling dissipated. The intensity of love let up.

I opened my eyes. The quail, congregated under the feeder, gurgled contentedly. A mourning dove flew squeakily over my head.

My inner conviction that Ruby visited me was totally illogical—I chided myself—but my heart had no doubt it was her. And no one had appeared before this, so I really hadn't expected anything to happen. My hands went up to support my newly heavy head, my tears slowed as I realized God had answered my prayers. I tried to stand, but I was dizzy, so I dropped back down and waited for it to pass. As I sat there, I remembered I never asked for validation—something Vickie always stressed to do when we made contact.

I decided to do it next time. *I actually believe there will be a next time.* I grinned just a little. Aunt Ruby had come to visit me! Everything was going to be all right.

I stabbed my fork at the chicken breast on my plate and pretended to concentrate on dinner. We were continuing our discussion from the night before. *I don't know how to explain to Ken why I'm going.* "I probably won't have another chance like this again. Besides, I've always wanted to see inside the hotel." I rearranged my broccoli before piercing a small floret and placing it in my mouth.

"One night is not worth a month of very bad days. You're probably doing this for nothing. *Nothing* will happen." His voice grew more insistent with frustration. "Think about how bad you'll feel. Please, don't put yourself through it."

I couldn't imagine how hard the past 18 years had been on him. The uncertainty. The loss of a partner who could hike, snowshoe or go dancing. In a way, my illness was harder on him than on me. It was more challenging to see a loved one so devastated by something he had no control over. At least I had power over my thoughts, my outlook.

Ken watched me. His fork lay on the cooling plate.

"You need to eat," I said, trying to buy time. I looked past Ken out to the grape arbor he'd made of white Romanesque columns. "Logically, I shouldn't go. You're right. This isn't good for my health. But I think of everything I've missed because of this stupid illness. And I'm sick of it. Yeah, probably nothing will happen. But I can say I went on a ghost hunt with paranormal investigators and a television news crew. How many people can say that? And, I'm doing this for work. Both Bill and Janice asked me to be there. This'll help us promote the conference...."

Ken scowled.

I continued. "Anyways, if nothing happens, it's still a great story to tell at cocktail parties."

"Except we never go to cocktail parties," he said, his hazel eyes saddened.

It was my last day of work before Goldfield. I stared at the computer screen trying to compose a press release on the upcoming Royal Father-Daughter Ball, when Anastasia, clad in a tailored, short skirt suit, knocked on my doorjamb.

"I want to wish you luck tomorrow." The former ballerina lowered herself gracefully onto the burgundy, aluminum-framed chair. "I don't want to sound like a mother hen, but I'm very worried about you. I saw a Sci-Fi Channel special on Goldfield last weekend. You know it's a scary, scary place. I couldn't even watch the whole show. Do you know about the murdered girl there?"

I held up my hand. "No, and please don't tell me. I don't want to know any of Goldfield's stories. I'm trying to be a good impartial observer. I can't plant anything in my brain." And it had been harder to do than I thought. One friend had wanted to loan me the book *You Can Never Leave Shirley* about the Goldfield's owners in the 1970s. Several people I knew had seen the *Ghost Adventurers* cable TV show where they featured the hotel. Others, upon learning I was going there, did Internet searches. It seemed every time I turned around, I had to say, "Don't tell me!"

"Well, you're brave. Braver than I am," she said.

"I'm certainly not. I don't think anything will happen."

"You'll be in my thoughts. Let's have lunch when you get back. I want to hear all about it. At least I think I want to hear...."

That evening, I packed bottled water and snacks in an ice chest for the inevitable 2 a.m. period when I'd realize it was just too long until breakfast. I made a mental note to cook up a can of chicken with rice soup and put it in a Thermos tomorrow morning. For clothing, I packed to dress in layers—a wool turtleneck, cardigan, coat, scarf, gloves, knit hat. I'd been told Goldfield was a cold place.

My plan was to stay up late that night, so I'd sleep later into the morning. I was to meet everyone at KTVN at 11 a.m.

Ken readied for bed. "Be careful. Those old buildings can be dangerous. Don't go anywhere that looks unsafe."

He kissed me and enveloped me in a big bear hug. He slipped his strong arms around my waist, sending shivers through my body. I pressed against his lean build, content. Nothing felt better than this.

"You really need to go to bed." Ken straightened the sheets and slid underneath.

"What's the point? I'll just toss and turn for hours." I stood by his bed. "Any way, if I stay up late, then perhaps I'll be able to sleep in."

"Just go to bed. You're more exhausted than usual. I see it in your face." He reached for my robe's belt and drew me close to him. He sat up and kissed me again. "Don't read your Bible tonight. Don't do crosswords. Go to bed."

"I will. Soon. I've got a few more things to do. I love you."

"Love you, too."

I was in bed by eleven and I dropped into an immediate solid sleep.

I'm in a light place. A meadow crammed with little purple daisies. My pain's gone. I run through the meadow, happy, carefree, with an enormous amount of energy. My limbs move freely. Gravity no longer constrains me. The sun shines in the crystalline sky. The weight of disease and financial struggles lift off me. I watch its dark shroud rise higher and higher into the heavens. Then I hear a loud voice. "You have to go through the dark with faith to get to the light. What you are doing has a purpose."

I awoke just then and lay in the dark. Calmness settled over me along with the distinct knowledge that everything was going to be okay. In my dream, I was healthy. I could run. I didn't hurt. My brain functioned. I wrapped the residue of the dream about me like a comfortable old blanket and fell back to sleep.

Ugh! I awoke at 7 a.m., way too early to pull an all-nighter. Ken was heading out for work. He stuck his head in the bedroom and jogged in to give me a goodbye peck. "Be careful. Have fun. Call me tomorrow and let me know how it went."

"I really don't think anything will happen. On the very off chance it does, I'll probably run out of the building screaming! Can you see the news promo? Bill saying, "Tonight at 11. Watch Kathy Berry lose her cool and race out of the Goldfield Hotel screaming her fool head off!"

"Finally! News worth watching." He kissed me again and left.

I pulled out my Bible and opened it randomly. It fell to John 1. I read:

> "In him was life, and that life was the light of men. The light
> shines in the darkness, but the darkness has not understood it."
> (NIV)

I recalled last night's dream where I'd been told I needed to have faith to get through the darkness and reach the light. I embraced my Bible. *Wow!* Another sign. God was with me. I'd be fine. I'd carry the light of faith within me.

It was one of those Nevada mornings when the sky's blue intensity mirrored Lake Tahoe's depths. I parked alongside a KTVN news van, its back hatch open.

A tall, lean man, probably in his thirties, pushed a large rectangular silver case into the back of the van.

"Are you Jeff Foss? I'm Kathy from TMCC."

His hair was slightly reddish and he had faint freckles. "Yeah. Great to meet you." The photographer threw a duffle into the van and turned to shake my hand. I think he was as excited as I was to embark on this adventure.

"Can you believe we're actually doing this?" I asked.

"No. But it should be fun. We've got room for you and your stuff in Kevin's car."

A red Suburban pulled up. Its front passenger window powered down.

"Hey, Kathy!" It's Cheryl with Ted and Janice. "Can you come over here?"

"Hi, guys."

"I've brought something for you. For protection. Make sure you ask me for it before we start the hunt tonight," Cheryl said as she twirled her locks with her finger.

"Thanks, but I've come to terms with this. I've decided there's a reason I'm going with you all."

Janice leaned toward the front seat and said, "Good for you!"

Cheryl smiled. "Of course there's a reason. You're going find tonight interesting."

Exiting the building, Bill greeted us in khaki safari-looking garb with a late twenty-something man, who I assume was Kevin Bennett, the young news producer. We all gathered behind the news van. The KTVN crew. The ghost investigators. And me.

Cheryl didn't offer protection to anyone else. I wondered if she thought I would be the one to freak.

I made a promise to myself right then that I wouldn't.

~12~
The Gem of the Desert

Goldfield Hotel. Photo by Ken M. Johns.

It's time. Bill holds the Goldfield Hotel's plywood-covered door open for me.

My palms sweat and my heart beats like a punk rock song. I have no idea what to expect. *Honestly, what really could happen tonight?* But just in case, I wear a cross under my t-shirt and the necklace Ken gave me the first Christmas we were together for luck.

It's going to be fine.

There's a purpose.

Nothing will happen.

My new mantras.

I recall last night's dream. Of feeling healthy, happy, energetic. Not the sluggish, weighted-down woman here at the doorstep. I wipe my palms along my slacks. "Thanks, Bill."

I step over the threshold. White dust blankets everything—black leather seats encircling brass and mahogany columns, abandoned sawhorses and a decrepit player piano. The floor's the worst: its intricate inch-wide, hexagon tiles forming white and black daisies barely visible under the filth. With each footstep, we sweep away the dirt, exposing our presence.

Goldfield Hotel lobby. Photo by Ken M. Johns.

The walls are partially painted, but the wainscoting and decorative ceiling beams have been removed, leaving naked, bone white lines across the walls and ceilings. The empty elevator shaft stands open: its black wood and glass doors etched with what looks like pineapples. I stop a foot from the open doors and bend over carefully. Below, there's water.

Everyone scatters to different areas of the lobby. Cheryl takes photos of the stairwell. Kevin, sporting a navy baseball cap, pokes at the dusty eroding keys of the player piano. Everyone talks at once; voices blend and echo off the walls. My brain short circuits. There's simply too much for my sickly mind to absorb.

Someone trips next to the mahogany front desk. "That was close!" I hear, though I'm not sure who says this as I'm mired in a cognitive fog. However, I feel relief it wasn't me stumbling in front of the camera. Someone laughs.

Janice comes up to me. "What do you think?"

"It's a cool building. I can imagine the women in their flowing white, bustled gowns and men in black suits and sophisticated hats. Thanks so much for encouraging me to come." In my mind's eye, I see fresh flowers and the diamond reflections thrown off by the light fixtures. I take a deep breath.

It's going to be okay.

We walk over to the reception desk.

Switchboard and room key cubby holes. Photo by Ken M. Johns.

"Bet you haven't seen anything like this before," Janice points to the telephone switchboard, its cords plugged in and ready for use.

"Bet I have! My mother was a department store switchboard operator when I was young."

"Well, this one probably hasn't been used since your mother was born. The hotel hasn't seen paying guests in more than 60 years. Can you imagine all of this closed for so many decades? Such a shame."

I'm tempted to touch this fragile piece of technology. But I don't. In a way, it's as if I'm in a museum. A forgotten one. Next to the switchboard is a gold-embossed wall safe. On the other side, the room key cubbyholes.

I lean against the front desk. A confusion of white brochures litters its mahogany top, gold lettering proclaimed the 1980s reopening of this splendid Gem of the Desert. I open one and see a big-haired professional woman in a red business suit lounging with a gentleman on the circular leather couch. The sales piece touts a long line of amenities including a video arcade, casino, indoor pool and spa, gift shop, gourmet restaurant, coffee shop and even an RV park. I read the headline, "Step into the color, the excitement, the fervor of the past."

Virginia, the caretaker, approaches us. Her hair is short—but not severe—a practical style for the Nevada desert. "These arrived from the printer the same time the renovation costs soared and the owner ran out of money," she says with a slight remnant of a southern accent. "We were only a few months away from opening. We were already booked solid for the first month."

Kevin motions to Virginia. "What can you tell me about this old safe?"

As she turns to face him, Janice takes my elbow and leads me in the opposite direction. "Come with me," she whispers. "I want you to see something…without anyone else around."

I search Janice's face. Her sparse, soft wrinkles. Her curled brownish-red hair framing her kind features. She winks at me and leads me out of the lobby and through another room.

"Maybe we shouldn't go. Bill wants us to stay together," I say in hushed tones, looking over my shoulder. Bill's speaking with Jeff. He doesn't see us leave. We turn the corner.

"Nonsense." Her eyes sparkle with mischief. "It's still light. We'll just be a moment. I want you to experience this." She stops at a small, dark room with a boarded-up window. Room 109. "Here. Go in."

I wonder what she thinks I'll sense. *She'll never understand I'm not psychic.* My eyes adjust slowly. There's a radiator near the bottom of one wall and a metal twin bed frame. As I stand in this dark small room, sadness showers upon me. I want to cry. Not mist up, but break into actual sobs. *What's got into me?*

"I knew it. You can feel it, can't you? The sadness." Janice studies me. "You do!" It seems she's standing a bit taller.

I can't feel her joy. "I want to cry." I search the room only decorated with a few stubborn scraps of wallpaper. "What's going on? Why am I feeling so desperate?" I swallow hard and will my eyes to stay dry. "Do others feel sad in here?"

"Those who are sensitive do. You see, this is Elizabeth's Room. You're picking up on her feelings. The desolation at losing her baby—"

Elizabeth's room. Photo by Ken M. Johns.

"Kathy. Janice. Where are you?" Bill hollers.

"Take a left at the hall," I yell back. I'd really like a few minutes alone to gather myself. Could I really be feeling the emotions of someone who stayed here a century ago? There must be another explanation. I feel as though I've been plunged into an extreme PMS mood swing, yet my cycle is nowhere near that stage. Perhaps I'm reacting to all the stress of coming and just being exhausted. Maybe it's just a coincidence this depression happened when I entered this room. Then I think of Vickie and how she said, "There are no coincidences."

The group's footsteps and banter get nearer. *I can't cry. I have to be professional.* I try refocusing, hoping Bill won't be angry Janice and I broke a rule we all agreed on. He wanted us all together for two reasons—for safety and if something unworldly should happen, it would get caught on tape.

But even the guilt of breaking a rule can't keep me from fighting this crushing depression. The desolation. The loss. The pointlessness of living. Then I come to a realization. *These feelings aren't mine.*

Silently, I ask if someone's here. If she feels this devastated. If so, I want her to know I'm sorry she's so miserable. I don't get any response, but then why would I think I'd get one?

The group arrives. Virginia's the first to step inside with us. "You've come to visit with Elizabeth?"

I nod. I'm afraid if I speak, I'll weep.

"That's nice. I try to visit her every few days. She gets very lonely." The petite woman says this as if it's the most normal thing in the world to visit a ghost.

Bill speaks up. "Is this the room where the young pregnant woman had been chained to the radiator?"

How horrible! No wonder she's so distraught.

Virginia nods. "Please give me some room. I want to put her at ease." Janice and I back to the wall as we watch the bespectacled 74-year-old drop to the dirty linoleum floor and sit crossed-legged in one graceful sweeping move, a feat I know I couldn't accomplish.

I hold back a sigh and will myself to cheer up. Bill, Ted and Cheryl inch into the room. The TV camera light illuminates the center of the room.

Virginia talks as the rest of us fall silent. "Honey—Elizabeth, it's me. I'm sorry I haven't visited in a while. It's just been so busy." Her face has changed. It's younger. Her wrinkles have eased and she appears completely at peace. "Yes. These people are here to visit you. Will you show yourself to them?" She pauses and cocks her head to the side as if she's listening to someone. "If you don't feel like it, we'll understand." Pause. "Okay," she coos softly, then turns to us. "She's uncomfortable. She says there are too many people in her room. Can y'all step outside into the hall? I think she'll show herself better if you do."

As I exit the room, the cloak of sadness lifts and I'm back to myself again. Could I have put myself through these emotions on my own? At any time, did I hear Elizabeth's story, lodging it into my subconscious? No. I'd gone out of my way to avoid all the hotel's ghost stories. About all I had heard was a woman haunted a room—but I didn't know the details.

We crowd in the hall just outside the doorway as Virginia resumes her side of the conversation. "See, I told you they'd listen…Why don't you move near the corner, they could get a better view of you there…No, I promise. I'll visit you more often… I do. I know how lonely you get—" She turns her head to the group. "Look, she's showing herself. Thank you, dear. That's great. See her up near the ceiling. You can see a soft light—that's her." Virginia's thin, bony finger points upward.

I study the spot she's pointing to, but see nothing. I take a photo. Just in case. Ted and Cheryl run their digital voice recorders while Jeff shoots video.

Virginia's strange one-sided conversation draws me in. I'm touched by the poignancy in the way she speaks to Elizabeth—like a beloved lost daughter returned home. She appears genuine. But my skeptical side raises questions. Could Virginia be an amazing actress who can convincingly hold her side of an unheard conversation? Is she mentally off? Or is Elizabeth indeed speaking to her?

I realize I want it to be true. I shake my head. We've been here less than a half hour and I'm already losing my impartiality.

I follow Janice across the hall to a larger room.

"Do you know Elizabeth's story?" she asks in a low voice.

I shake my head.

"She was just a teenager. They say George Wingfield was her lover."

"Didn't Wingfield own this hotel?"

"Yes. He did. But I'm not sure he's the father of her child. He didn't live here long. He moved to Reno early on. Others just say her lover was very prominent in Goldfield. That he chained her to the radiator to prevent a public scandal. Someone would bring her food and other necessities. You wonder why others would allow this to happen. All I can figure is the man was so powerful, no one would stand up against him." She strolls over to an empty closet and glances inside.

I think of news stories where people walk by someone hit by a car or beaten by a thug and do nothing to help. Perhaps humans have always had a bad side, not wanting to put themselves at risk even if it means sacrificing someone else. Then I think of the infant. "What happened to the baby?"

She slowly walks the perimeter of the room. "I've heard many stories. Some say it died in childbirth. Others say it was given up for adoption. The worst tale I've heard, though, is the baby was snatched from Elizabeth's arms, and then thrown down the mine shaft in the basement of this building."

"That's horrible!" I imagine Elizabeth's desperation. Her empty, outstretched arms.

"It's said there are times when you can hear a baby cry down there. I've never heard it though."

I go to the room's uncovered window and stare at the brick wall of the building next-door. "I hope it's just an urban myth. What happened to Elizabeth?"

"Oh, there's a bunch of stories surrounding her too. Some say she was released. Others say she died in childbirth. Or, perhaps, she was murdered. I've tried to do some research, but it's difficult, since no one seems to have her last name. I can't corroborate anything. I just know something very bad happened in room 109."

"I can believe that," I mutter.

"Virginia told me that in the 1970s this room still had a padlock on the outside of the door. Now what's the point when there's a lock on the knob? One would surmise you would only put a padlock on a door to keep someone from getting out."

Jeff turns off the camera light.

Such a tragic story. One that could easily grow into folklore. Logically, the whole scenario sounds far-fetched. If there was a padlock, why would she be chained to the radiator? There's a small bathroom in the room, but it would take an extremely long chain to allow her to use the facilities. And, I assume, the hotel would have been in operation. So if she screamed or yelled someone should've heard her. "It's hard to believe it could happen," I say. I pause as a thought comes to me. "If everything was kept so secret, how did this story get out?"

"I've asked that too. Some of the details come from the townspeople who say Elizabeth's story has been passed down through the generations. It was originally told by those who helped keep Elizabeth sequestered and felt badly about it. Other details have been brought to light by psychics."

My heart goes out to Elizabeth. Whatever happened to her. The only thing I'm sure of is the absolute, overpowering desolation and hopelessness in her room. A sensation that vanished as soon as I stepped out, feeling like a distant memory. Yet one, I believe, I'll remember for a long time.

Virginia leads Bill, Kevin and me up the central wooden staircase to the Vortex Room on the south side of the second floor.

"Did you know this hotel holds one of the seven vortexes?" Virginia asks. "You know, like the one in Sedona. Except ours is inside a building."

"Yeah, I read that when I researched the hotel," Bill answers. "So how does it contribute to the hotel's paranormal activity?"

Virginia keeps up with Bill's lengthy stride. "A vortex is a portal. A door between the spirit realm and our world. Ghosts can come and go as they please. That's why there are so many spirits here at any given time."

Ghostly portals. *Really? How preposterous!*

We reach the second floor. The corridor is long. I flash on a scene from *The Shining*. We pass one empty room after another, each doorframe edged in dark, once-polished wood. In its most recent incomplete renovation, workers removed the guest room doors. Sunlight filters in from the windows, checkering the linoleum floor.

"Here we are," Virginia says once we reach the end of the hall.

I'm disappointed by its normalcy—it's just a bare room. Like any other on this floor. I'm not sure what I expected. *Neon lights announcing, "Ghosts enter here?"* Bill, Kevin and I exchange glances—I sense they're a bit let down as well.

"Okay. Close your eyes and reach out your hands in front of you,"

Virginia says. Bill and Kevin comply, so I do too. "Good. Now walk slowly to the window."

I imagine how we look, the three of us. Perhaps like zombies creeping along with our arms outstretched. I listen to our footsteps, hoping I don't run into Bill or Kevin. I concentrate on moving in a straight line toward the south-facing window. My hands feel the slight presence of electricity.

"My hands are tingling," Bill says.

"Yes. Good. That's the energy the vortex puts out," Virginia says with a slight twang. She pauses. "Okay. Stop and open your eyes." Bill and Kevin face the window. I'd veered slightly to the left.

"Well darn it. Normally everyone turns left and ends up facing the corner, where the vortex is." She sounds disappointed as if we are disobedient children. "Okay, Bill, let's try something different." She brushes her palms back and forth. "Rub your hands together, then reach out toward me—but don't touch me."

He does, then just as quickly retracts his hands. "Ohhh, weird. I feel pressure. Like you were touching me."

Virginia smiles. "I've knocked down a burly man in this room without ever coming in contact with him."

As the impartial observer, I mull over what could cause the tingling sensations we felt. I wonder about high-tension power lines and look out the original glass window. "I don't see any electrical lines outside. Is there any other kind of power source nearby?" I ask.

"Nothing. The energy you feel—" She stops at the sound of our group stomping up the main stairwell. We wait for their arrival. The clopping stops at the second floor landing. No one appears.

Bill glances at us, shrugs and checks his watch. "Maybe they decided not to bother us. They're probably telling us it's time to get to the gas station, so we can eat dinner before it closes."

The Dusty Fender Grill and Fill is the only restaurant and gas station in town. They stop serving at 6 p.m. Since it will be our last hot meal for the next 13 hours or so, we immediately head back to the first floor.

No one waits for us at the stairwell. This doesn't sit well with me, but it takes me a moment to realize why. Then I know. The footsteps never retreated or continued up the flights. They reached our floor and stopped. No voices. No people. I shake off this irrational thought.

As we corner the final landing, I note everyone's where they were when we'd left them. Jeff still works on his camera. Ted, Cheryl and Janice are deep in discussion at the circular leather couch. A shiver runs through my body.

"Why didn't you guys come all the way?" Bill asks.

The group stops chatting. Their faces blank. Jeff looks up from his gear. "What do you mean 'all the way?'" he asks.

Bill's eyes widen. "We heard you on the steps. We thought you wanted to see the Vortex Room."

"We haven't gone anywhere since you left," Jeff says.

Bill laughs deeply, spontaneously. Whether it is from nerves or excitement, I can't tell. "It's not even dark, and they're already letting us know they're here!"

So it starts. My belief this will be a quiet, uneventful night dissipates. I finger my cross and think of my dream last night. How there is a purpose to this. I look around the once-opulent lobby. I'm not scared. However, I am unsettled. I can't trick myself into believing nothing will happen tonight. Bill is right. If they're letting us know they're here and it's still daylight, what will they do tonight to make their presence known?

Dinner no longer sounds appetizing.

~13~
Séance

The fried chicken salad I ate for dinner sits in a wad in my stomach. I lie on the bed at the Santa Fe Motel, an early '70s, several-room establishment located more than a mile away from the Goldfield Hotel and Highway 95. Adrenaline courses through my body, giving me an artificial energy I'll pay dearly for tomorrow. I rest anyway, trying to conserve what I can for the evening.

Everyone's taking a break before we immerse ourselves in the ghost hunt. Janice's in the shower. Ted's taking a walk. Cheryl's at the sink trying to tame her hair. The TV from KTVN's room mumbles through our walls.

Cheryl, holding a large barrette between her teeth, brushes her hair.

I prop myself up on my elbow and raise the pillow so it cradles my head against the plastic veneer headboard. "What got you into all this?"

She pulls up the hair on each side and holds it in place with one hand, while she grabs the barrette and secures the hair at the crown of her head. "When Teddy and I were young, we lived next to a cemetery and I'd see these strange people wander among the tombstones. It probably wouldn't have been bad if the spirits stayed in the cemetery. But they didn't. They'd come into our house. No one in my family noticed them. Except for me. You can't imagine my fright at seeing things no one else saw."

She grabs a purple paisley scarf off the counter and wraps it loosely around her neck and flips the ends through a loop to keep it in place.

I've always hated cemeteries. I'd lose it if I ever saw a ghost in a graveyard. Of course, I can't tell Cheryl that. I have to come across as self-assured and brave. After all, I'm not going to freak. "Yeah, I bet. How frightening."

She grabs her overnight bag and then looks up at me through the mirror. "But it's more than that. No one believes you. My mother told me nothing was there. But I saw them. Even Teddy didn't believe me. I bet he was 16 or so before he believed I was psychic. Of course, it helped that a spirit I saw actually touched him." Her body shakes with her full-throttled laugh, a wild contrast to her soft, feminine voice.

"Anyway, after Teddy returned from his tour in Iraq, we shared a duplex. We'd heard about electronic voice phenomena and decided to try it. We found out we were pretty good at getting it. We've even gotten EVP on our front porch! But the main reason we do, is to help others, especially parents who've lost a child. You know, being able to help them by contacting their loved ones who've passed over."

Cheryl stares into the mirror, not at me, but to a faraway place. She's saddened.

I wonder if I should say something, but I don't know her well enough to pry.

She shakes her head slowly, as if clearing her mind and sighs. She roots around in her overnight bag, looking for something. "Ah, here it is," she says, extracting a tube of mascara.

She strokes her eyelashes with the wand. Her large green eyes look wet.

I stare at the popcorn ceiling and wonder what tragic destination she'd traveled to.

She clears her throat and stands tall. "You know you'll be all right tonight. I'll be looking after you." Cheryl returns the mascara to the bag, and then pinches her cheeks to add color.

"Thank you. I really appreciate it. It unnerves me not knowing what to expect or what my reaction will be if something should happen."

"There's no way of knowing that. Make sure to put out positivity. If you do that, you'll receive good, spiritual responses. If you put out fear, then guess what'll happen? You'll attract fear. But, and I mean this, you'll be just fine. Really."

I feel bad about her earlier offer of a gift. For thinking it meant she assumed I would freak. Cheryl has a good heart. "You said you had something for me, for protection?"

"Oh, you don't need it anymore. You're going to do fine." She zips the bag closed and tosses it into her open suitcase on the bed.

The full moon peeks over the hotel roof. Large, glowing white. *What will this great orb witness tonight?*

At dinner, Cheryl suggested the spirits were more active when the moon showed its fullest. I didn't understand why, but nothing about the paranormal has made any sense to me, so I had let it go.

I feel a bite to the night air despite wearing a wool turtleneck and bulky sweater. I go to the open back of the news van to fish out my coat.

The prevailing quiet on this weeknight permeates the surroundings, penetrating my soul. Nothing—not even a stray dog—stirs except for us. I don't know what to hope for. A substantial part of me still believes spending the night in a haunted hotel is ludicrous. Kitschy. Odd. Almost humorous. With my coat zipped, I join part of our group gathered under the lone streetlight on the corner.

"I saw her. I tell you, I did," says Billy, the carpenter who worked on the hotel during its last renovation. The group's huddled around him. "She was blonde. Real pretty. Wearing a long white dress, as they did back then. Walked out of her room then down the hall."

"Was it Elizabeth?" Bill asked.

"It sure was. She came out of her room. I'm telling you, she caused me a whole lot of troubles. I'd fix something and the next day it'd be broke again." He smiles broadly, exposing teeth sorely in need of a dentist. Earlier, Billy told us he'd left his job in Los Angeles not knowing where he would go. But when he reached Goldfield, he felt he belonged.

"Well, it'd be great if we could see Elizabeth tonight," Bill says. "Even better if we catch her on tape."

I shudder. I don't want to see an apparition. The shadow man had unnerved me enough. And I don't ever want to see him again. My stomach flutters. *I'm in control. Everything's going to be all right.*

"The studio lights should be set up soon," Bill says. "We appreciate the extension cords and access to your power, Ruth."

Ruth, an explosives expert who's rebuilding Goldfield one building at a time, smiles. Her latest project is renovating the old bank building next door. "My pleasure. You'll be glad to have at least one well-lit area tonight. Anyway, Billy and I appreciate the invitation to take part in the séance. We've never done anything like this before."

Just then, the lights pop on in the hotel lobby, liquid gold spilling out the open front door. Like moths, we migrate to it.

Kevin comes to the door as we get there. "Why don't we bring in the rest of our supplies?"

So, we provision our base camp: the lobby. Sleeping bags. Ice chests. Camera gear. Sacks of food. Coats. Inflated mattresses. Flashlights and lanterns. Backpacks with our personal supplies. With my arms full, I enter the half-lit lobby, its outskirts blanketed by the night. An island of refuge, surrounded by nothing but blackness. I avoid looking into the dark, hurrying outside to grab more gear.

Take control. Whatever's here can't hurt me. So what if ghosts march up steps and people talk to them? I'll be fine.

With everything and everyone inside, Bill closes the front door. Kevin breathes deeply, repeatedly into one of the air mattresses. Jeff's snapping open cases and extracting camera gear. Ted fusses over his video equipment, checking batteries and such. The rest converse near the elevator.

I place my pack near a circular couch and take off my coat, suddenly feeling warm. I find a quiet place next to the front desk, act as if I'm looking at something of interest and whisper the Lord's Prayer...*but deliver us from evil. For thine is the kingdom, and the power and the glory forever. Amen.*

I'll be okay. God's seen me through too much—18 years of illness, thoughts of suicide, and life in general—to let something bad happen to me now. Anyway, I do carry the comfort of the Lord's signs: the dream, Aunt Ruby's visit and the Bible verse. I recall its words, "there is light in the darkness." I must remember to carry Jesus' light within me.

Cheryl approaches, fingering a palm-sized digital voice recorder with her long black fingernails. A small white ghost is painted on each tip. This frivolity helps put me a little more at ease.

"How're you doing?" She rubs her palm against my upper arm, carefully pulling back her nails so she won't snag my sweater.

"Fine. I guess. Nervous, actually."

"Remember what I told you." Her large emerald eyes stare deep into mine. "You'll get out of this what you put into it. You must have faith in yourself."

"Thanks." We head back towards the group.

"Wanna do some EVP with me in the bar until they finish setting up? I'll give you a quick lesson."

"Sure." I go to my pack, extract my Mag-Lite—a black flashlight longer than my forearm. Its heft comforts me. Like I'm carrying a weapon. I chuckle as I imagine myself swiping at apparitions.

Electronic voice phenomena sounds so far out there to me, even with my new and improved open mind. During a past ghost conference, an EVP specialist shared his evidence of life after death.

"Here's a nice recording I captured when I visited a castle in Wales. Now, listen closely."

He pushed a button on his laptop. "MRNMNRRMR."

"Isn't that something? You can clearly hear the spirit say 'Yes, I'm here.'" He paused. "Let's hear it again. 'MRNMNRRMR'…. See how clearly the spirit's voice came across!"

I tried not to roll my eyes as heads nodded around me, thinking they heard a ghost's voice.

Cheryl and I depart the illuminated sanctuary, past the decaying player piano and into the lounge. As we do, I realize I'm holding my breath. I must remember to breathe tonight.

"Did you hear Billy say this bar tilted off the ground?" Cheryl asks.

"Yeah. It's amazing what you'll see after seven or eight beers," I quip.

She positions herself at the end of the bar. "I've seen weirder things. Come help me lift this."

We push, pull, heave. Nothing budges the 12-foot-plus bar.

"Billy just wanted something good to say on camera." My head pounds. I'm weak from the momentary exertion.

"You know if a spirit really used the surrounding energy, he could probably move it." She pulls the recorder out of the pocket of her tunic. "The most important thing about EVP is to treat the spirits as people. Show them the same respect you would for any person. Another important tip: Once we start recording, stay very quiet. Don't walk around. Don't make any noise. If you want to ask a question, just give me a sign."

"Sounds good."

"Let's do it." She pushes Record. "Hi. Please excuse us for barging in. I'm Cheryl and this is Kathy. We're here to learn about you. I'm holding a voice recorder. You may use the energy, noise from this device, to communicate with us. Please speak with us. Please."

I'm taken aback by how polite she is to probably nothing. It would've never occurred to me to introduce myself to an empty room. Perhaps, though, Cheryl sees we're not alone.

"Can you please give us your name?" She pauses to allow time for a response. "We were told you can lift this bar. It's very heavy. Did you really do this?" Quiet. "Did it make you unhappy they were going to reopen this hotel?" Silence. "Would you lift the bar for us?" We wait. "Please don't feel like you need to perform for us; we'd just like to verify your presence."

She holds up her palm to me and we stand there silently. The recorder's little red light pulses on and off. She clicks a button and the light disappears. "Let's see if they had anything to say." She hits Play. It's a voice-activated recorder, and all we hear is Cheryl's voice. "Damn. Nothing. Let's try over here." She points to the darkest corner of the saloon.

I flip on my flashlight to illuminate our path.

Once again, she introduces us and apologizes for interrupting. "We'd love for you to speak with us….Please share anything you'd like with us. We're here to learn…."

She presses Play. This time, I hear a strange noise after Cheryl speaks. More than white noise. Louder.

"Great! We got something," she says. She replays it again, this time to her ear. "I can't make out what he's saying, can you?"

She holds the recorder to my ear, its metal casing cold against my head. It's a weird noise; one we didn't make. Fast, rhythmic static. Not a voice. I shake my head.

"I've got to put this on the computer. Sometimes we slow a voice down, so we can understand what they're saying…I'll save this one." She pushes a button.

Cheryl heads to the doorway. I follow like a toddler close on Mom's heels.

I peer into the lobby, the studio lights so bright, they hurt my eyes.

Bill and Janice set up the séance, spreading white Glad trash bags in a circle on the floor since we don't have any furniture to sit on.

"We've got time for one more. Let's try over there." She points to the lounge's farthest corner.

I doubt we'll get anything that'll resemble a voice.

She repeats her opening, then asks a couple questions. She holds the recorder out between us as she pushes Play.

I hear something like "itch" followed by a growl-like noise. At least that's how it sounds. "I hear something!" I say. "He has an itch!"

Her face is featureless in the dark. But when she speaks, she sounds cautious. "Good catch, Kathy. But that's not what he's saying."

"What did you hear?"

"He said, 'Bitch. Leave.'" Her voice says this slowly, calmly.

Why would a ghost say that? Cheryl was perfectly polite. I hug myself, unsure what to do.

"Listen." She places the recorder up against my ear, but it's the same to me…the word "itch" followed by a strange growl. I guess it could've been 'Bitch. Leave.' Fear builds inside me. Something doesn't want us here. I clench the edge of my coat. "We better tell Bill—we need to leave this room." I turn, but Cheryl takes a gentle hold on my arm.

"It's okay. Really," she says, almost cooing. "We just startled him. But we should go. It's time for the séance."

As we walk out, I whisper, "I'm so sorry we disturbed you." Then I tell myself nothing had recorded and try to convince myself no one told us to leave.

Bill looks about the lighted room, rubbing his hands together. "We're ready, folks. Is everyone sure they want to take part in the séance?"

I nod a bit reluctantly.

Billy the carpenter, Ruth the explosives maven, Kevin, Cheryl and Janice all say "yes."

Ted stands there with his hands in his pockets.

"You don't want to participate, Ted?" Bill asks.

"I've had a bad experience with seances. I'd prefer not to." He steps away from the circle.

Great! Someone who delves into the paranormal is too scared to be in a séance I've agreed to participate in! I contemplate changing my answer, but don't want to appear afraid.

"Oh, Teddy! You said you would," Cheryl says, reprimanding him.

Bill chimes in, his voice upbeat. "No problem. We have enough people for it. You can help me observe and Jeff will man the camera."

I whisper to Janice, "What happened?"

"Something took possession of him. He talked in a strange voice and when he came out of it, he couldn't remember anything he said."

"Oh." I look at Janice's calm face. I trust her friendship and push down the fright and the gas station dinner that once again works its way up to my throat. Vickie said I could handle this. So did Cheryl. I'm in control. God will protect me. I cling to these thoughts as I pick a white trash bag that backs to a wall. For some reason, this makes me feel a little better. As if a ghost needs an entryway to appear!

Everyone sits Indian-style on the floor. Vickie had said crossing one's legs or arms shields one from spirit contact. So, I gladly join the others, crossing my legs in front of me.

Cheryl pushes her scarf out of the way as she lights three votive candles and places them in the center of the circle. Bill turns off the studio lights. It's just the light from the TV camera and the candles. Ruth sits to my right, Kevin to my left.

"Okay everyone. Let's turn our left palms up, right palms down and hold each others' hands," Cheryl instructs. "I'll get us started, but if any of you have any sensation, feeling or even if something pops into your head, please let us know. Everything can be a message. Also, try to be as open and accepting as possible to help us get a better response. Bill? Can you grab those cigars?"

He grabs them off the sawhorse and hands them to her. She places the tobacco cylinders perpendicular to each other beside the votives. "Ah, good. This is an offering to them," she says.

"To whom," asks Ruth.

"The spirits," Cheryl replies.

An offering to something other than God! A Christian shouldn't be here. Silently, I pray for the white light of protection and for forgiveness. I tune out everything—exactly what I shouldn't be doing. I sit there so walled up, I don't even hear the conversation. After a while, I realize there's no point to being here if I intentionally close my mind and my heart. So I work on being more open, accepting and putting out positivity.

"I'm getting the name Grady," Janice says. The candle's flicker falls short of her face, until the camera light fully illuminates her. "Does Grady mean anything to anyone here?"

Billy speaks up. "Grady lived in Goldfield for a long time. He passed away several years ago."

"Okay. Billy, why don't you talk to Grady? Ask him a question," Janice suggests.

Just then, Billy's head snaps up. "Look! Over there—" He points to the saloon entrance. "A cowboy!"

In the excitement, someone exclaims, "I see him, too!"

Slowly I bring my eyes up to the doorway, but all I see are Bill and Jeff's backs as they run into the lounge.

With the camera in the other room, our only light emanates from the three votives. I close my eyes, not trusting my senses or imagination.

"Hold on. I'm getting something," Cheryl says. "There are lots of spirits here. They're watching us. Spirits, how many of you are in this room?"

It's silent except for Bill and Jeff's footsteps in the saloon and Billy's hard breathing.

"Fourteen. There are fourteen of them." Cheryl laughs, splitting the quiet with her mirth. "They think we're entertaining them, putting on a show for their benefit."

Several people chuckle. I muster the courage to look about me. Just darkness.

Ruth speaks up. "It's strange, but I just got a clear picture of an opera. We were on the stage. They're telling us we're like watching an opera!"

Yeah, right. Perhaps, they've got their wires crossed. But, I must admit, part of me is intrigued at the thought of ghosts being entertained.

My shoulders fall back into place and the stomach butterflies dissipate. I open myself up further, trying to be welcoming to any message I might receive. I'm startled by how quickly it happens...a whiff of sweet cologne. Old-fashioned toilet water. It's overpowering and fills my sinuses and then just as quickly, vaporizes.

"Anyone wearing perfume?" I ask.

The women shake their heads.

"I smelled perfume. It came on suddenly, almost overwhelming, then it was gone."

"Good job, Kathy. You picked up on a spirit," Cheryl says. "That's why you don't wear perfume to a ghost hunt. The spirits can tap any of our senses."

Even with the short time I've spent in this building, I've encountered spirits in three unique ways—hearing the footsteps, feeling Elizabeth's emotions and now smelling a woman's perfume. And it's only 10:30 p.m.

A very small part of me—infinitesimally tiny—starts to look forward to what else the night will bring.

~14~
Voices

11:25 p.m. The real investigation gets underway. We're back to our original group of seven as Ruth and Billy returned to their homes and warm beds. The chill sets in, so I zip my coat to my chin. We gather around Bill, our group's alpha member, in the hotel lobby.

"Let's set some ground rules. First—everyone needs to stay together. From time-to-time, we can break off into two groups, but no smaller. I don't want anyone panicking and getting hurt."

Everyone nods. Bill's excitement has subsided. He looks serious. I wonder if he's nervous as well or just wearing his reporter face.

He continues, "When EVP's being conducted, someone say 'recording.' Then, let's stand completely quiet. I want as accurate a recording as possible. Also, please keep in mind this is journalistic inquiry—and if nothing happens, that's as valid to me as something happening. We don't want manufactured drama." He claps his hands. "Let's roll!" Bill isn't smiling. *He is nervous!*

I practically attach myself to Janice's side as we stride into the saloon where the ghost told Cheryl and me to leave.

"Recording!" Ted announces.

We stop. Listen.

My flashlight chases after every sound and creak around me, yet I hope I won't see anything. I wonder: *What would a ghost really look like*? A slightly formed mist? A transparent human figure? Someone who looked alive? Or worse—someone who appeared dead? *Why did I come here?* I place the Mag-Lite between my knees and wipe my sweaty palms along my thighs.

All we document is loud white noise. There's no sign of the "Bitch Guy." I watch Janice, Ted and Cheryl record, play, rewind and sometimes save, if they believe they have something to pull out with the computer.

Next, we investigate the ballroom/dining area, the northern-most room on the first floor. The windows facing Highway 95 are boarded up except for large portions of exposed plate glass where it's too high for someone to reach. Occasionally, a car drives through town, splashing high beams across the walls, slashing the darkness.

The Goldfield's ballroom. Photo by Ken M. Johns.

"Hey, everyone," Bill says as he leans over a grand piano. "I'm going to see if this still plays." The camera's on as Bill plays "Chopsticks."

We cheer and clap. He laughs.

"Did anyone see that?" Cheryl shouts over the din. "In the doorway to the basement stairs. The Cowboy. Did anyone else see him?"

Immediately, all lights close in on the stairwell. I snug myself between Janice and the wall, eliminating the space around me. The Cowboy, who was supposedly seen by Billy during the séance, is said to be a resident ghost here.

"Take a photo, Kathy. Take it of the doorway," Janice urges.

I snap a shot. When it pops on my screen, odd red, green and yellow squiggly lines hover in the upper portion of the entry. *Oh my God. What is that?*

"Let's go after him," Cheryl says.

"Yes. We were heading there anyway," Bill replies.

Let's not go into the basement! I say to myself. But it's either go or be left behind, so there's no choice. I force my way into the middle of the procession, having no desire to be among the first into the basement or among the last to stay in the ballroom. I want to hold someone's hand. I need human contact.

Everyone else seems calm. And, although this is a strange assignment, it's still work-related. I don't want to do anything to jeopardize my relationship with KTVN. I have to hold on to some degree of professionalism.

We creep down the concrete steps in the tight service stairwell. I train my light on my sneakers.

The confining basement is a concrete maze of narrow halls. Pipes run across the low ceilings. And, it's frigid down here. Freezing, claustrophobic, gray and black.

"A dark movement—in the hall to the left!" Bill's voice is higher than normal.

"I see it too!" Janice exclaims.

"Where?" Kevin asks.

"Half way down," Bill says.

"Boy, it was quick," Janice adds.

I encourage my eyes to look up, but they stare at my feet instead.

"It's gone. It was blacker than the black around it. I saw it move," Bill exclaimed. I look at him, his face pale, his demeanor not quite as self-assured. He really does look as if he's seen a ghost.

"It's a shadow person," Cheryl says, matter-of-factly. "They're all over this building."

What a comforting thought! I think of my history with shadow people, the fright of seeing them. My past panic. I chide myself. After all, I'm in control, I tell myself. I'm with others. And I'll stay positive. Even if it kills me!

Our first stop in the basement is in a room that supposedly houses a water well. Ted notices part of the floor is dirt. He digs around with his foot and finds a metal panel. "I bet this is it," he says.

"I hear this well has spiritual components," Cheryl says, almost to herself.

"Recording." Ted looks about to make sure we heard. "Hi, I'm Ted. These are my friends and we're hoping to communicate with you." He pauses. "We're not trying to get you to perform for us. We're just trying to learn about spirits." We all stand quietly. "Did anyone die in here?" Silence. "Okay. Let's see if we got anything."

He pushes Play. We listen to Ted's stoic voice on the recorder. "…We're just trying to learn about spirits. TTTTDDD IIIILLKKTHT."

Everyone looks at each other. Cheryl says, "You got something!"

He plays it back. "TTTTDDD IIIILLKKTHT." I hear the same garbled noise.

Cheryl says, "He's saying, 'Ted, I like that!' Play it again."

"TTTTDDD IIIILLKKTHT."

Janice chimes in, "I think you're right."

I, on the other hand, don't hear a voice or words. But, I admit, it was a different sound. One our team hadn't made during the recording.

Bill says, "Can you play it again? I'd like to hold it to my ear." Ted hands it to him. Bill nods after it is done. "It could be. It might be a voice. I just don't know."

Ted replies, "This one will clean up nicely on the computer."

"Thanks. Why don't we head to the room where they say the brick was thrown?" Bill turns to Janice. "Do you know where it happened?

"Yes. In the old barbershop."

"I'd like to find the shadow person down the hall," Ted says. "Does anyone want to go with me?"

Kevin heads over to Ted. "I will." Jeff also joins them.

There's no way I'm going to go hunt for a shadow person. "I'd like to go to the brick room myself," I work to keep my voice level.

So, Bill, Janice, Cheryl and I head over to the corner room outfitted with a hexagon-tiled floor and a bricked-up entrance against the outer wall. This room is particularly cold. I marvel that Cheryl's only wearing a jean jacket over her light tunic and canvas pants and Janice has on a gray University of Nevada sweatshirt. I place my flashlight between my knees and shove my hands into my coat pockets.

Janice must've seen me looking at the walled up door. "There was an outside entrance to the barbershop. The men took these stairs to get here. Women weren't allowed. It was purely a man's domain."

"I'm sure the women felt they missed out," I say a bit sarcastically. I spy a pile of bricks on the floor along the outer wall. Sheet rock and lumber are stacked against the room's perimeter. It's small enough that our flashlights and lanterns illuminate it entirely. I lean against a wall and let the light sink into my consciousness. I feel safe here.

"When *Ghost Adventures* came here," Janice says, "they started yelling, hoping the ghosts would react. They never expected to get a brick flying through the air towards them."

"I saw the same episode," Bill says. "They claimed experts verified the authenticity of the footage. But the video was somewhat dark and not quite focused."

"I'm not convinced it happened," Cheryl chimes in. "It takes a lot of energy to hurl something that heavy. It looked like something unseen threw it. Let's see if we can learn more. Recording." She begins her introductions.

Bill and I freeze in place, so we don't complicate the EVP recording. Jeff quietly walks in and starts filming. Ted and Kevin remain down the hall scouting for the shadow person.

Cheryl continues speaking into the recorder. "There were some men here that weren't nice to you. They insulted you. Yelled at you. On their TV show, they show a brick thrown at them. Honestly, I don't believe you guys did this." She quiets and glances at each of us. "But if it did happen, can you let us know who did it?" Pause. "Please, if you guys did it, can you tell me on the recorder that you did it?" Quiet.

Janice nods to Cheryl, indicating that she wants to ask a question.

"Then you can say to us, look what we've done." Silence.

Cheryl resumes. "Or if you did it, can you throw another brick across the room?" Pause. "No. I'm sorry. That's too much to ask."

We stand there like statues.

"How 'bout if you move a little bit of plaster, something easy, just to show us you're here?" Silence.

Janice nods to Cheryl again. "But, nothing to hurt anybody."

Cheryl coughs, and then continues. "We just want to know you exist."

She stops recording, then presses Play. "Hi, I'm Cheryl and we...."

I think how brave Ted and Kevin are to have chased after the shadow person and am relieved to be in a fully lighted room with no shadows.

"...Can you throw another brick across the room?"

"No thank you, we've already done that."

We gasp in unison.

I'm stunned. A male voice. One that doesn't belong to Bill or Jeff.

Oh my God. A ghost is here with us!

"Did you hear that? DID YOU HEAR THAT!" Cheryl throws her arms in the air. "Ahhh, man, I've got chills. Teddy. Teddy," she yells. "I have Class A!"

I look about me. I don't feel a presence. No eyes upon me. Wouldn't I feel something in this room, if there really was a ghost? But the voice was clear. Something's in here with us. Then it hits me. *I've heard a spirit speak and I'm not scared!*

"Cheryl, please play it again," Bill says.

We huddle around her and the recorder. She plays it back. "Thank you, but we've already done that." The voice sounds surprisingly pleasant.

Wow! Spirits can be polite! "Ohhh. Astounding! Thank you so much. Thank you." I say to the room, not knowing where to look.

"Yes. Thank you!" Bill says.

"Teddy. Kevin." Cheryl calls down the hall from the doorway. "You've got to hear this."

"What constitutes a Class A?" Bill asks.

"The clearest EVP. One you can understand without cleaning up or slowing down," Janice replies.

I just can't believe it. How I easily understood the voice. How polite it—no, he was.

She replays it. Enormous gratitude and awe build in me. This room feels safe to me, more so than the others. And this is the room with the ghost. How extraordinary it is that he made an effort to communicate with us. I think of Vickie, "Spirits are people without bodies." I get it, really get it now.

Ted and Kevin rush in. "What's the fuss about?" Ted asks.

"Class A, Teddy. We've gotten Class A!" Cheryl chants almost like a cheerleader. She holds out the recorder and pushes Play. Ted breaks into a smile, the first one I've witnessed with him.

"Hear it?" Bill asks Kevin.

"Maybe," he says as he slightly shakes his head.

The ghost's voice has an odd staccato cadence; there's no way it could be mistaken for a human voice. I look about me, actually willing this polite gentleman from the past to appear, but see nothing. I wonder if he's still around, amusedly watching our reactions.

Bill laughs. "Well, I did! And I can tell you, no one in this room said it—at least no one living! Let's see if he has anything else to say."

Cheryl hits the Play button once again. We huddle around her, so close I can feel the warmth of my comrades. Her recorded voice continues. "How 'bout if you move a little bit of plaster, something easy, just to show us you're here."

Another voice. This time a woman's. "Didn't mean to hurt anybody."

I shake my head. Did I really hear her?

Cheryl's recorded cough. Then Cheryl's final recorded statement. "We just want to know you exist."

We all stare at each other. I can tell by everyone else's faces that they heard her, too.

"Another voice!" Cheryl exclaims. "Another Class A!" She high fives Teddy.

I am in the presence of a man and woman long dead who want to talk to us! And, amazingly, I'm not frightened. Blessed. Privileged. The last thing I would've imagined experiencing right now.

Wow. Ghosts and spirits do exist. And this isn't Hollywood. They can be polite, remorseful. People without bodies who interact with us beyond the grave. Who want to converse with us!

My views on reality evaporate into a fine mist.

I look at this objectively. Play the devil's advocate. Could Cheryl have recorded the two voices earlier? I discount this as I've seen them repeatedly record and erase the recorders in the dark all night. Then, it occurs to me Cheryl's cough was on the recorder as well as Janice's voice. They sounded exactly the same way as it happened. Then there's the matter of their excitement. The ghost hunters were as astounded as we were. So my brief skepticism dissipates into the night's chill.

We're all laughing. Patting each other on the shoulder as if we've done something great.

"If we get nothing else, this has made the trip," Bill says. "Wow." His face is one huge smile.

Quietly, I say thank you again. What a revelation. Over no more than two minutes max, I received proof the soul lives on. That it doesn't exist in a lonely void. And that spirits can be around us, even if we don't feel them. They want to reach out to us, communicate with us.

My fear of ghosts transforms to awe.

~15~
A Sympathetic Stranger

As I stride out of the Voices Room, staring down the long dark hall daring something to appear, I know I can handle anything no matter how bizarre or unworldly. Well, that is, at least at this moment. After all, spirits are just people without bodies. *So what's there to fear?*

Alas, no specters appear. We stop in various rooms with no measurable results. One room just like the other. Windowless. Cold. Concrete. Quiet as a tomb. Then in one such room, Cheryl's hands fall limp to her sides.

"Why are you showing me this?" she utters to the wall, her voice shaking.

We glance at each other. It's obvious she isn't speaking to us.

Ted goes to her and places his hand on her shoulder.

She stares where the floor meets the wall. "No!"

It's the first time I've seen her calm demeanor shattered.

"Sis?" Ted lightly shakes her.

She turns to him as if she doesn't realize he's there—her large eyes magnified. "I have to go upstairs. Call home. Now." She bolts.

Ted chases her.

The rest of us stand there unsure of what happened.

Bill shrugs. "I guess now's as good a time as any to take a break."

We trudge up the basement stairs through the ballroom and saloon to the lobby, our lights trained on our path.

Entering the lobby, we break into our own small islands of solitude to give Cheryl some space. I pick a dusty wooden bench near the front door, the excitement of the Voices Room set aside for the moment.

Cheryl rifles through her backpack. "Where's my damned phone?"

"I've got mine handy, if you want it," Janice offers. She hovers near Ted and Cheryl.

"I know it's here, let me look a little more."

Ted says, "I'm sure everything's okay."

She doesn't look up as she pulls out a sweatshirt and throws it on the dirty black leather seat, along with batteries, a hair brush and a pile of other items. "You didn't see the dead cat, Ted. Why would there be a dead cat in the basement! Here's the phone." A tinny song emanates from the device as she turns it on. "I'm not getting many bars. Oh, please let me have service...."

"We'll get service, even if I have to drive to Tonopah." His voice stays soothing.

Immediately, we all go to where we stashed our phones and turn them on. I'm still not sure what's happening, but I really hope one of us can get service.

"Oh, here it goes. One more bar...Thank God, I've got service." Her long fingernails fumble with the buttons. "Come on. Come on. Pick up. Where is she?"

I look to Janice, who says, "She must be calling her pet sitter."

"I'm super sorry to wake you up. I know it's late...No everything's fine. But—but can you please check on my cat?" Her voice is shaky and her New York accent more pronounced. Ted stays by her side, standing at attention. Cheryl whispers, "She's looking for him." She shifts from one foot to the other in a nervous dance.

No one says anything. It's an intensely private moment, one I'm sorry she has to share with us. I want to fade back into the wall. Various team members sort through their belongings or adjust their equipment. Everyone averts their eyes.

"You found him? You're sure he's okay?... Thanks so much...I'm so sorry to have wakened you. Thank you again. See you Friday." She shakes her head as she flips the phone shut and flops onto the dirty leather seat. "My cat's fine. He was asleep. I can't figure out why a spirit would show me a dead cat. Maybe he was just messing with me."

Two weeks later, I read an obscure biography—loaned to me by a friend whose relatives knew the Goldfield Hotel's owners in the late 1970s. They wrote about one winter when their cat had died and the ground had been so frozen they had to put the carcass somewhere until the spring thaw. They'd stored the deceased cat in the basement.

With the tension relieved, we break out some snacks and kick back. Janice joins me at the wooden bench against the wall. Everyone's chatting in little groups.

"So what's Ken think about you doing this?" She takes a bite of a red delicious.

"He didn't want me to come." I unwrap a protein bar.

"Because he doesn't believe in the paranormal?"

"No." I lower my voice so the others won't overhear. "It's because of my health. He's afraid tonight will tailspin me into a worse exacerbation. He said I'd be doing everything that triggers an attack."

"Really? Like what?" She sets her apple down on a napkin on her lap and looks at me with motherly concern.

"Adrenaline. Standing for long periods. Going to bed late, or worse, not going to bed at all."

"Maybe this time will be different?" She dabs her mouth, looking at me hopefully.

I frown. "With my health, I never get away with anything." I think of the conversation I had with Ken just the night before. How he's probably worried about me all day. I picture him curled up sound asleep with the covers completely covering his head. So far, I'm doing pretty well. But I shudder at what I'll feel like later once the adrenaline crashes.

Janice sets her hand on my shoulder. "I wouldn't have asked you to come if I'd known this would cause you problems."

"No. I'm glad you did. It's been amazing so far and it's just a little after 1:30! Who knows what else will happen? Really. I can't thank you enough for encouraging me. You know, there are times I just have to do something and not worry about the consequences. I hate living my life working 25 hours a week and staying in bed the rest of the time. I've missed out on so much." The anger pushes up out of my deepest recesses, the resentment of so many years lost. "Using all my energy for work, then not having anything left to do what I really want. Fun things, you know, like hiking with Ken, going out with friends, spending time with my niece and nephew. Writing. I'm sick of all the time I spend in bed or on the couch, feeling too lousy to be bored. I resent that Ken doesn't have the active, fun girlfriend he used to. I don't want life to continue to pass me by. Tonight's worth it. It's worth a month or so of feeling much worse—"

I lose my train of thought. Someone touches my head. The light pressure of a hand running from my crown down the back of my head. Open fingers parting my hair in an unmistakable sensation. A tender, stroking motion of solace.

I go rigid, but I'm not frightened. It's soothing, a caress. But logic dictates that this is impossible. I look about me. No one's to my left side where I'm being stroked. It isn't Janice, as she's to my right, and the rest of the team's snacking and talking among themselves. Behind me's just the wall. Nothing juts out. The surface is smooth. It's got to be my imagination or some rational explanation.

The sensation ends. The unseen fingers no longer linger on my head. Cautiously, I raise my hands and pat the top of my skull. Nothing's there. I run my fingers through my hair. No bugs.

Janice lifts her hand off my shoulder and looks at me suspiciously. "What's wrong?"

I lean toward her and whisper. "Something patted my head." Not a real accurate description, but I don't feel comfortable going into details about it. It sounds too weird.

She smiles so I can just about see every molar. "The team needs to know. This is great. You realize that, don't you?"

"You think they'll believe me?"

She nods.

"Okay. I guess… go ahead." I don't have the courage myself to make the announcement.

"Everyone! A spirit just touched Kathy!"

The group quiets and stares at me—and I worry about what they're thinking. *Is she crazy? Is she looking for attention?* There's no way to prove this. Even among this open-minded group, I hope no one judges me.

"I'm sure of what I felt. It wasn't in my mind," I stammer. "I wasn't even thinking about ghosts at all when this happened." And I hadn't been. I was considering my health and the steep price I would pay for tonight. A thought occurs to me. The spirit must've eavesdropped on our conversation. Perhaps she was trying to offer support or express her sympathy. The timing was just too coincidental. Once again, I hear Vickie's voice, "there are no coincidences."

Cheryl bends down next to me. She hands me the recorder. "Push this button. And ask the spirit if it touched you." She smiles encouragingly.

Everyone's watching me. No one's talking. I fidget in my seat, clear my throat and speak into the palm-sized device. "Hi, this is Kathy. Did you just touch my head?" I pause only briefly, and then erupt into nervous giggles. *Great. I can't even get one little EVP recording right.*

I pass it back to Cheryl. She hits Play. "Did you just touch my head? YSSS." Then my giggles. "I get a 'yes' Kathy!" she says.

I do hear something. Something short. It sounds like a "yes." I want it to be a yes. I can't tell whether it's a man or woman's voice. But that doesn't matter.

"You know, Kathy, the spirits really like you." Cheryl grabs a mini white zinfandel from the ice chest.

"Really? Thanks." I don't know what else to say. It seems an odd concept that ghosts could like somebody. Then I think of the alternative. *I wouldn't want the spirits to hate me.*

What a gift this entity gave me in showing her compassion for me. For wanting to console me through touch. How amazing God is to find a way for an ethereal being to convey support, and in a way, hope.

I smile, imagining a spirit nosy enough to eavesdrop on our conversation. Curious, perhaps about our lives and who we are. *Gee, how far from Hollywood horror flicks can you get?*

~16~
Thumps in the Night

"I've heard a bird in the house is a bad omen," Bill says ahead of me as we climb the central staircase. "A dead one must be even worse." He steps over a pigeon corpse—its white and gray feathers forever grounded.

I take a large step over it as well, trying not to notice its eyeless face nor think of this poor creature flying on, never locating its escape.

My butterflies are gone. I cling to how positive the spirits have been. But even thinking this, my intuition feels something else waits for me.

On the dark second floor, I fully comprehend the concept of "spooky." Spooky is a long dark hallway with dozens of gaping doorways to pass by. Passages that aren't always staggered: some openings face others across the hall. As I pass those entrances with their darkly finished mahogany frames, I don't know whether to look to my left or to my right. If I gaze one way is something peering at me from the other? I banish the thought.

Stay positive, I remind myself. *They have done nothing bad, only good.* Besides, Cheryl told me I'd get back what I send out. So armed with my prayer of protection, I won't dwell on the negative or evil.

Just south of the central staircase near the Vortex Room, I catch a whiff of lilac. "Mmmm. Smells good," I say without thinking.

Janice, who is just behind me, senses it as well. "Ah. The Lilac Lady. She's come to visit."

Our procession stops, but the scent vanishes. I wonder if the fleeting aroma means the lady has fled as well.

"Did anyone else besides me and Kathy smell lilacs?" Janice asks.

Everyone shakes their heads "no."

"The Lilac Lady is a resident ghost here. She stays in this area and her calling card is always the same: her perfume."

Each member of the group takes turns walking the small stretch of hall where the perfume revealed itself. No one else smells it. After a few minutes of unproductive EVP, we move on.

As I enter each room, I excuse myself for interrupting. In many of them, I feel a presence—whether there's someone there or it's just my imagination after so many paranormal happenings, I don't know. Regardless, I apologize for intruding, take a couple of photos and proceed to the next naked room.

Goldfield Hotel guest room. Photo by Ken M. Johns.

We tramp on like schoolchildren—a bit tentative and in single file—on our way to class. Our flashlights create little globes of light floating from the floor to a noise to a room. Constantly moving.

As we reach the corner near the Vortex Room, Janice stops and snugs her ear to the wall. "A woman's singing. Does anybody else hear her?"

Cheryl goes to the wall, cocks her head. "Yes. Yes, I do."

"It's coming from this room," Janice says.

This guest room's different as it actually has a door.

Janice attempts to turn the knob. It won't budge. "It's locked. Why, of all the rooms here, does this one have a door? And why's it locked?"

"Not just locked," Bill says as he runs his fingers along the jamb. "It's been sealed."

"Makes me want to get in all the more," Janice replies. She and Cheryl jog over to the room next to the inaccessible chamber.

I tag along.

They stand in a bathroom that actually has a sink and toilet. They press their ears to the wall.
"Nothing," Cheryl says.

I wish I could've heard the singing. Yet another thing I'd never guess a spirit would do. "Did you guys hear actual words? Was it an upbeat tune?" I ask.

"Slower," Janice says. "I couldn't make out any words. I wish we could've gotten in there."

We join the others in a nondescript, stripped-down guest room a few doorways down the hall.

"Recording," Cheryl says and then goes into her spiel. She pauses and points the recorder at me. I shake my head. I wouldn't know what to say. She resumes her questioning. I'm getting tired and am not paying much attention, when all of a sudden, there's the sound of knocking.

Not a tentative rap, but an urgent prolonged banging.

"Hear that?" Bill asks. "Let's find where it's coming from."

We fan out along the dark hall, looking around us, but the noise doesn't happen again. One thing I know for sure, it wasn't the building settling or a natural noise. I guess it's possible someone knocked on the front door downstairs, but we're at the far north end of the second floor and I doubt anyone would have the strength to produce such a clear sound so far away.

Goldfield Hotel hallway. Photo by Ken M. Johns.

On the third floor landing, Bill momentarily freezes, then points down the hall. "There. Look! A shadow person. Second door on the left." His voice, up an octave, is little more than a whisper. "Someone's peering around the corner at us. Someone short!"

I stare at the empty, sanded-down doorway, marveling that Bill has seen two different shadow people. Why haven't I seen anything?

"It's a child," Cheryl states. "Don't be afraid, little one. We just want to meet you," she says in a motherly fashion while slowly ambling to where Bill pointed.

"A kid. Of course!" Bill says.

All the flashlights converge on the doorway.

I wouldn't mind seeing a shadow kid. Maybe it'd be a good baby step for me. Get used to the little shadow tots and then maybe when I see a shadow adult, I won't scream my fool head off!

By the time everyone gathers at the doorway, the EVP recorders are going. Some of us stand in single file. In front of me, Kevin shivers. "Suddenly, I'm cold."

As I start to reply, the cold wave hits me. *Something's moving by us.* As soon as I acknowledge the temperature change, it returns to normal. One more odd sensation in an unusual evening.

Next, Janice, Cheryl and I enter a guest room. It carries a heaviness, an overwhelming sense of foreboding.

"Oooh, I don't like this." Cheryl strides straight into the bathroom, as if she has a psychic inkling. She stands near the window for a moment. "Ohhh!" She rushes out. "Something tried to push me. Push me out that window. I don't like this. I don't like this at all….Go in there…let me know if you feel anything," she says to both of us.

Go in? She thinks something wants to kill her and she wants us to enter that bathroom? I don't move. I let Janice go instead.

"No, this isn't good," Janice says. "Something bad happened here." She rotates in a circle, taking in every inch of the bathroom. "It feels dangerous….Kathy, why don't you come in here and give it a try?"

Great. It's dangerous. Such an invitation.

Janice exits and sweeps her hand toward the room. I stand at the bathroom's entrance and push all negativity out of my mind. I ask for a white light of protection and tentatively step inside. Every muscle in my body tightens. I look around. Besides a rust-stained sink, there are no fixtures. A gaping hole with wires protrudes where the light would be. And the room really needs to be painted. It hasn't been updated as recently as those on the second floor. I try to open up. A pit forms in my stomach. But I wouldn't say anything's trying to kill me.

"What do you feel?" Cheryl asks.

I exit the bathroom. "Anxious. But I'm not sure if I would've picked up anything, because I knew what you guys experienced."

Right then, Kevin strolls by the room, his lantern hanging low at the end of his arm. Cheryl calls to him. "Can you tell us if you feel anything in this bathroom?"

"Sure." The young television producer marches into the lavatory without hesitation. Now Kevin is the biggest skeptic in our group, so I'm curious to what he'll sense. "Oh. OH! Not good." He bolts out. "I don't like it." He's pale. "What happened in there?"

Bill hears us. "What's happening?" I hear the kid in him saying, "I wanna play too!" He comes in and looks at his boss. "Are you all right?"

Kevin replies, "Go into the bathroom."

We all watch, wait. Bill goes in, turns about and exits. His eyes are wide. "It was strange. Like I couldn't breathe."

It's amazing how we all perceive different things; none of us experience the same sensations as anyone else. Kevin wasn't sure about the basement voices, but from the look on his face, I could tell this room disturbed him.

Later, I read there had been a suicide on the third floor. Some man jumped out the window. I wonder about him; I've little doubt someone died there, but it wasn't suicide at all. Based on the experiences of our group, I'd say it was murder.

We gather at the northwest corner of the third floor where Ted and Jeff conduct EVP. Ted asks the spirits, "Have you been here long?"

We stop in our tracks so we don't interfere with the recording. The full moon shines through the western windows, providing us with a comforting light.

Ted pauses. "Why do you come here?" Quiet. He stops the recorder and puts it to his ear. His eyes shift to Cheryl.

He frowns and hands the device to his sister. She listens and grimaces as well. She shuts off the recorder and returns it to Ted.

Her seriousness compels us to stay quiet.

He returns the recorder to his pocket. "We need to leave this floor. Now. They don't want us here. They want us to leave. We must respect their wishes. Let's get to the fourth floor."

Cheryl nods in agreement.

Gee, when Cheryl heard "Bitch Leave" in the saloon, she didn't worry. Why is this different? I want to ask, but Ted ushers us down the hall. Perhaps we're in danger. My heart thumps. It's all I can hear. As I turn toward the service stairwell, I catch Cheryl leaving a cigar in the room. I wait for her at the landing and hope she hurries, as I can no longer see the rest of the group.

"Why did you leave the cigar?"

"This is where the Cowboy's supposed to hang out," she explains as we go up the last flight of crumbling concrete stairs. "I want him to know we don't mean any harm."

So, the cigar's an appeasement. I wonder if it is a gift to the spirit, so it doesn't hurt us. *Stop the negativity!*

On the fourth floor, I survey the area. No renovations have taken place here in decades. Bare, skeletal walls reveal dry timber studs surrounded by a thick white, rope-like material. It's breezy, quite cold. I pull up my coat collar and snap it closed around my neck. The windows are broken; some are paneless while others have large triangular glass shards jutting out the wood frames.

It would be up here, amid the decay, that I would get my biggest fright of the night.

"The little boy. He's up here now." Cheryl's talking fast, excited. "I hear him. Playing. I need to find him." She starts combing the rooms, calling out to the boy in a voice only a mom would use.

I hear Ted in a nearby room and go find him, as I don't want to be alone. Even for a moment. So much for the bravado I felt after the Voices Room.

"Where's Cheryl?" he asks.
"She heard the little boy. It's so sad he's here by himself. Wouldn't he be afraid and lonely?"

Ted's eyes widen a bit. "Why do you assume he's by himself? Their world isn't much different from ours. Spirits don't exist in a vacuum. There are others who look out for him."

Ahh. This makes sense. The 14 ghosts watching the séance. The two people in the Voices Room. They like company just as much as we do.
"I'm beginning to see that," I say. Since I have Ted to myself, I ask him about the third floor. "What did the spirits tell you downstairs? Did they threaten us? Is that why we had to leave?"

He turns from the broken window. "No. We were making them nervous. I believe they were afraid of us. And we don't want to scare them." He pats my shoulder.

They're afraid of us? Who knew humans could make ghosts uncomfortable!

"I better go find Cheryl. She has a soft spot for kids. One of these days, she'll make a great Mom." Ted leaves me alone in the hall, so I scramble to find the rest of the group.

I see moving lights in the corner room. I find Janice, Bill and Jeff in a guest room lacking plasterboard and a ceiling, as Janice conducts EVP.

I want to lie down. Now. My head feels like a bowling ball and my legs like spaghetti. My overloaded senses can't take any more bizarre experiences that challenge logic. Deep down, I know I can't take one more thing, one more experience crammed into my already stuffed brain. I need to stop ghost hunting and go to a non-haunted place. I'd go to sleep. At least I think I could.

Cheryl and Ted rejoin us. With our entire group once again assembled, we turn the corner to traverse the last long corridor for the night.

Wing beats echo overhead. A bat swoops down over Janice and Cheryl. Janice shrieks. Cheryl ducks and covers her head. I can't help but grin. These people who aren't afraid of ghosts are scared of bats.

It flies down the hall and into some distant room.

Ted, Cheryl, Janice and Kevin head to the opposite end of the building.

I start to follow, but Jeff calls to me. "Can you give me a hand with lighting? My battery's getting weak and I need more light to shoot up here. Could you walk in front of me and shine your flashlight?"

That's how I ended up at the head of the line, after working so diligently to be in the middle of every group. It's after 3:30 a.m. and my brain is shutting down—how can a rational person reconcile so many strange, yet amazing happenings? I stumble around in a fog, trying to concentrate on holding the light where Jeff directs. I've given up looking toward every little sound and peering through every gaping doorway.

Behind me, Jeff and Bill converse, but my brain doesn't register what they're saying.

I'm exhausted. I pray silently, "Please let nothing else happen tonight. I've experienced enough." My dry eyes ache from the dust. And I've been on adrenaline far too long. *Give me a bed, a couch. Let me lie down in a well-lit modern motel room. Hell, let me lie down in the news van!*

Jeff is behind me to my right. Bill, behind to my left. The others' flashlights spill out of a room at the far end of the building. A world away.

As I reach the top of the central staircase, something charges me. Heavy, fleet steps. It's someone big. Football player big. Rushing up the last flight of stairs. At me. I yelp. Loudly. I brace myself for the inevitable bulldozing, tightening every muscle and planting my feet. I swing around to eye my pursuer. Shine my light at the stairs. No one's there. The footfalls stop abruptly. Nothing collides into me.

I scan the staircase with my Mag-Lite. It's empty. I shake uncontrollably and hold back the tears. I knew no one would be there. I drop the flashlight to my side.

Bill yells, "WE HAVE MOVEMENT! Come quick."

I pry my eyes off the vacant stairwell. Bill is plastered against the wall at the landing. His eyes narrow. His mouth stern. I briefly wonder if he's mad I screamed out. I just stand there, unable to move. Unable to speak.

He takes his lantern and goes down the steps to the third floor and returns. "No one's there." He says aloud more to himself, than Jeff and I. "No one's there."

The others run toward us. I'm numb and don't look up. Janice slips an arm around me. "You okay?"

I lean into her.

Bill tells them something ran up the steps. I see the EVP recorders out. Camera flashes cutting the darkness. Someone talks about knocking sounds. Knocking from the neighboring elevator shaft. Lots of voices. Nothing sinks in. My body shuts down. Time stops. I can't handle any more. The footfalls weren't so much scary as they were startling, like a teenager lunging at a child in a cheesy Halloween haunted house. Except I'm not laughing.

Even with the nice, polite spirits, it's too much to comprehend, to process mentally, emotionally and rationally. My stamina's gone.

~17~
Floating Darkness

I don't remember anything else about the fourth floor. I imagine we went in and out of the other guest rooms. Perhaps some little incidents occurred, but I don't register any of it.

Back in the lighted lobby, I sigh and flop down on the inflatable mattress; dust poufs out from underneath the side as I land. It's 4 a.m. Not much longer to go.

Ted goes into Elizabeth's room to get the video camera he'd set up before we went upstairs.

Everyone keeps to themselves. No one's talking when Ted returns.

"The camera battery's dead. Nothing recorded." He goes to his pack and unzips it.

"I know we charged both of the batteries," Cheryl says.

"I'll try the other one." He pulls out the extra battery, inserts it and turns it on. "Now it's working." He heads back to Elizabeth's room. Jeff accompanies him.

"I'm thinking we're just about done tonight," Bill says. "But, I'd like us to try one more thing. We'll sit in a circle with our backs to each other, turn out the lights and just look around. Then we can go back to the Santa Fe and crash. It'd be good if we could get a few hours of sleep before investigating the World War II airbase this afternoon."

I want to beg to him, "No more! Please. Let's go to the Santa Fe now." A warm room. Pillows. Blankets. Not haunted. Sounds like heaven. But I don't voice my opposition as it's not my investigation and I'm just the impartial observer.

"Good idea," Cheryl exclaims.

Ted and Jeff return to the lobby, Ted with his tripod and video camera resting on his shoulder. "She just won't let me do it. Elizabeth doesn't want the camera to work!"

Cheryl smiles slightly.

"The camera was working fine just a minute ago. Then, as soon as I get into her room, the battery shows dead. When I leave her room, the camera comes back on and the battery's fine."

"She's zapping the energy from your equipment," Cheryl says with a hint of amusement.

"Ya think?" Ted says, then his face softens. "Sorry. I was hoping to get her on tape."

I can't grasp the notion of a ghost zapping a camera's power supply. But I know they've zapped mine.

"We're all tired. Let's finish up," Bill says.

We push two air mattresses together and sit along the edges, facing out in all directions.

With my feet squarely on the floor, my knees almost hit my chest. I sit facing the hotel's front desk. As each person sits upon the mattress, airwaves ripple and bump us. My hands are cold, so I put them in my pockets. Bill is next to me, sitting toward the hallway that leads to another hall to Elizabeth's room. Even Jeff has put down the camera to join us. Kevin extinguishes the lights. I suppress a whimper and close my eyes.

"Let's stay quiet, unless you see something. Then tell us what you see and where it is," Bill says.

My eyes remain closed. I don't want to play anymore. And no one can see I'm cheating.

"I see a shadow moving near the elevator," Cheryl says.

Quiet.

"I see a shadow going back and forth in front of the hallway," Bill says.

Silence.

I'm feeling guilty about having my eyes closed, so I open one at a time and just try to will "things" away.

A semi rumbles along Highway 95, its brakes squealing as it passes the hotel.

"I think I might have seen something move near the stairs," Kevin says.

My eyes adjust; I can just make out the front desk's silhouette.

Soundless.

I see a blackness lacking definition, but having a strange unity to its impermeability. It floats up near the ceiling between the front desk and Bill's hallway. I don't like it. I don't like it at all, but I'm numb and can't react anymore. It seems to move with a purpose. Unlike a dust mote in a sun's ray, it moves in a straight path toward Elizabeth's hallway. "I see darkness floating. It's moving to your hall entrance, Bill."

"Yeah. I keep seeing black things move around that area."

Quiet.

Then there's a sound. I can't quite make it out. It's coming from the elevator shaft.

"Hear that?" Cheryl says quickly. "A woman's voice."

Everyone must hear something as we all mutter at the same time. Someone says, "She must be in the basement. It's coming up the elevator shaft."

"I've got to go." Janice hops up and runs from the lobby, her footsteps plod through the saloon and, I imagine, on into the basement.

"Wait! You can't go by yourself!" Cheryl exclaims, jumping up from the air mattress to accompany her.

I don't know what to do. This is crazy! Janice hears something in the basement and she runs after it? I start thinking of all the horror movies I've seen, where someone hears a noise and goes into the basement. Like someone would do that in real life! But now, on the floor of the Goldfield Hotel after 4 a.m., life indeed plays out like a B movie.

The rest of us fidget; clothes rustle and the mattress jostles with movement.

Kevin speaks up. "I can't let two women go into the basement alone. Especially without a flashlight." He turns on a studio light, grabs a flashlight and runs after Cheryl and Janice.

That leaves four of us. *I AM NOT GOING DOWN INTO THE BASEMENT.*

Ted stands. "I'll see what's going on."

Three of us remain. Shoot! If everyone else goes, I'll have to, too, because there's no way I'd stay in this room by myself, especially after seeing that floating black thing.

I look to Bill and Jeff. Bill shakes his head. "I can't believe Janice just did that."

I let out a weak chuckle. "It's like a horror movie. Don't go into the basement, Janice. Then she hops up and leaves! I have a new respect for those stupid films."

Kevin returns. "Everyone's fine. Janice never went into the basement. She said she saw something and wanted to follow it. She and Cheryl are in the ballroom."

Janice, Cheryl and Ted laugh as they enter the lobby.

"Janice, what made you run out?" Bill's voice sounds tired.

"I saw the Stabber Ghost," she says matter-of-factly.

"The what? What's a Stabber Ghost?" I ask, not completely sure I want to know.

"He's one of the resident ghosts here. He runs around with a knife and stabs at people. Of course, he doesn't hurt anyone. I think he's just joking around. I saw him near the saloon entrance. I wanted to get closer to him. I followed him into the ballroom, but then he disappeared."

A stabber ghost. *Lovely.* I'm glad this is the first I've heard of him.

I look at my watch: 4:35 a.m.

"Well, what do you think?" Bill asks. "Shall we call it a night?"

"Yes!" I say without hesitation.

Everyone concurs.

I unplug the mattress and lay on it to let out the air.

We pack everything up, and then take it out to the vehicles. All that's left are the studio lights.

Our last official act of the evening is to take the group photo. I stand next to Janice at the edge of the group. As the flash goes off, I feel as if someone's standing next to me, posing with us. I acknowledge the presence silently and hope something shows up on the image. But it doesn't.

At 4:46 a.m., I walk out of the Goldfield Hotel for the last time. And I send all the spirits of this Gem of the Desert a weary thank you.

~18~
Heaven and Hell

Slipping under the covers of a cheap motel bed never felt this wonderful. With my body and mind beyond exhaustion, I melt into the stale, cigarette-smelling mattress as if I'm part of it.

Janice, Ted, Cheryl and I share one room at the Santa Fe. I'm hoping we all fall asleep quickly and wake late. Janice—who insists I take a bed just for myself (I'm sure she dug in because of my health)—is changing clothes in the bathroom. Ted has stepped out to give us a little privacy and Cheryl braids her hair. I wear a denim-colored, scooped neck, cotton nightgown, the one I wore in the hospital after neurosurgery.

Cheryl comes to sit on the edge of my bed.

"You handled yourself well tonight."

I take her hand and squeeze it. "Thanks. Yeah, I can't believe I did so well. It helps having you guys here."

"Janice and I were worried. We thought the spirits would play tricks on you. But they liked you. Oh, that reminds me." She walks back to her suitcase and pulls out a leather strip with a fabric square sporting a painting of a Catholic saint. "I was going to give you this for protection. I know you didn't need it, but I bought it with you in mind. So—" She hands it to me. "Just in case you ever need a little extra help."

"Thanks for thinking of me." I finger the leather strap and cup the saint's painting in my other hand. "Thank you."

Ted cracks opens the front door. "Is it safe for me to come in?"

Just then, Janice exits the bathroom in her flannel PJs. "Come on in!" she says.

Ted locks the door behind him.

I say my thank yous and goodnights, turn off the light over my bed, and close my eyes.

Unfortunately, Ted, Janice and Cheryl are hyper, yammering on and on about the basement EVP. How good it is. That it confirms the brick throwing. I'm so tired right now, I really don't care about anything. I pull the sheets over my head to tune them out, but little snippets still filter through to my brain.

"Can you get out the recorder? I want to hear it again," says Janice.

"Listen to this. Just listen!" Cheryl exclaims. "I can't believe it's so clear."

"This could open doors for us," Ted says.

"We're not in it for that," Cheryl chides.

And so it went, on and on. In a way, it was great to hear their enthusiasm. To know I heard special EVP. But I can't deal with anything. I want to sleep. I place a pillow over my head to drown out their banter and the light.

At 5:42 a.m., I can't take any more. "PLEASE! Go to bed. I really, REALLY need to sleep and I can't with all the talking."

Janice speaks up. "Oh, dear. Of course. We're very sorry."

They lower their voices, whispering. A light or two turns off. I guess I fall asleep, because the next thing I see is the clock readout showing 7:27 a.m.

I'm wide-awake, listening to my roommates' soft breathing, watching the light filter through the slit between the brown curtains. I can't believe I'm already awake. We've got a full day ahead of us with another investigation, and I've gotten less than two hours sleep after being up almost 23 hours straight. I've got to go back to sleep or I'll be too sick to do anything today. I turn on my right side away from the crack in the drapes.

Relax. I take a deep breath and mentally count backwards. 100. Breathe. 99. Inhale. 98. I don't want to disclose my illness to everyone, which I'll have to do if I have to lie down in Kevin's SUV instead of partaking in the airbase investigation. I need to go back to sleep.

Shoot. Where was I? 97? 87? I breathe in deeply and start over. 100.

I flop around the bed to find a more comfortable position. I think of the basement voices. *Stop!* 96. Breathe. 95.

If I don't block out all thoughts of the Goldfield, I'll never get back to sleep. Inhale. 94. Exhale. As I listen to my roommates' deep slumbers, I'm surprised there's no snoring. 93. Breathe. 92.

I remember how it felt to have a ghost stroke my head. How lifelike the touch felt. How I wasn't afraid. Then I recall the entity rushing Bill and me on the stairs. How I braced for the slam that never came. The floating blackness moving about the lobby. Images, sensations, scents rush at me. My mind reels. It already seems so preposterous, so illogical.

Stop it. I must sleep. But it's useless as the gates of my mind awaken and my thoughts accelerate. I ponder all the entities teaming in the hotel. Elizabeth. The Cowboy. The now infamous Stabber Ghost. The Lilac Lady. The little boy. The Voices Room spirits. The 14 who attended the séance. And those were only the ones I heard about. A crowd. How the ghosts seemed to interact with each other and with us. How they had fun. How they were polite. They acted like regular people. Ted was right: most of the Goldfield's spirits didn't exist in a void.

Someone starts wheezing. Cheryl coughs, turns onto her stomach and falls back to sleep.

I wonder if during the séance, she was correct about us entertaining the 14 spirits. Like we performed for their enjoyment. If Cheryl did receive the message correctly, they showed us that even though they're dead, they still seek out company and enjoyment.

Heaven would be their oyster, traveling wherever they like, visiting whomever they choose. *Complete and total freedom without the constraints of a body!* No limitations imposed by a three-dimensional universe.

Wow. If I had such freedom, I'd travel to all the places I love: the tall grasses of the Serengeti, my childhood home in West Covina, the rugged landscapes of Alaska, the manmade majesty of the Parthenon. I'd also visit places I'd never been, but always wanted to see: Patagonia, Ireland, the pyramids of Egypt. Perhaps I could time travel: visit opulent Victorian London, the bustle of ancient Rome, the Jurassic period with its towering dinosaurs.

Yes. It would be bliss to do what I want, where I want and when I want to do it. Freedom without this broken-down body imprisoning my choices. Causing me pain. Condemning me to sit out most of my life. Perhaps I could fly, feel the breeze against my airborne soul, knowing I no longer faced any earth-bound limits.

I'd check in with my loved ones still on Earth. I'd cheer them on in their victories. Hold them up during their trials, sending every ounce of love I have for them, hoping a small part of their consciousness would feel my presence.

And, I'd spend time with those who passed before me, expressing my adoration to them as I never fully did when they were alive.

Just yesterday, Heaven was a quiet, sedate, pious place to me. In other words, blessed but boring.

Today, Goldfield's spirits have changed my view, as they were anything but staid. Some found us entertaining. Others sought interaction. I guess even the spirit that charged me may have been playing a practical joke. Hardly quiet or pious!

So why do I believe these spirits are in heaven and not somewhere else? I guess it's because many were having fun and came from a positive place. If the afterlife is good, it has to be with God.

But how can Paradise contain a dark, run-down hotel? I recall Cheryl telling me many spirits visit places where they spent memorable times. And they see a place as it had been when they first visited. So, I guess they'd see the Goldfield in its regal splendor.

As the spirits—in some cases—congregated together, I surmise they must enjoy company and fun. This would mean they still possess at least some emotion. So, if this theory's true, wouldn't the love they have for those left behind be an even stronger attraction for them? I think of my cherished ones who've passed on: George, Ruby, Uncle Allan, my grandparents. Wouldn't they come to check on me? Wouldn't they want to be near me? I realize I've probably been oblivious to visits from loved ones—as clueless as I'd been to the two spirits in the Voices Room.

Since the Great I Am is love, and the soul lives on, it dawns on me that the love we carry for others would accompany us to the afterlife. It wouldn't stay in the grave with our useless shells.

This revelation stifles any chance at additional sleep.

A noise emanates from KTVN's room—someone's running water in the bathroom. I sit up and stretch my arms.

While heaven seems a likely home for many of those we encountered last night, not all the spirits were happy. Specifically, Elizabeth. Abject sadness and desperation filled her room. Virginia said she gets lonely. Elizabeth is in hell.

Why? A thought occurs to me. Who can create the most horrific hell for each of us? We can. We're harder on ourselves than anyone else is. So, it figures that the Almighty allows us to make our own Hell.

Perhaps Elizabeth's afraid to account to God. Refusing to move on, repeatedly reliving her mistakes and her personal devastations. Maybe she believes it's a better alternative to facing the Great I Am's wrath. So she replays her sins, along with the imprisonment, shame, loneliness and the loss of her child without ever moving on, without ever going to the Lord's loving light.

I bet even the most dastardly, evil person must face some trepidation about meeting God—having to account for his/her deeds once the bodily draws of greed, power and perversity have been diminished by death.

I catch my breath as this insight reaches into the depths of my being. Hell isn't something imposed on us; it's something we create upon refusing to seek out God's love and redemption. Fear, guilt and stubbornness keep us rooted to the past, trapping us to relive our worst, most horrifying moments over and over again. This knowledge electrifies my heart, touching a chord resounding in truth.

I lie back down and stare at the popcorn ceiling, letting this revelation sink in. How different this perspective is from my previous beliefs. I'd thought the Lord condemned us to hell if we hadn't lived a good, righteous life. I shudder with the realization that a hell of my own making would be mountains worse than the physical discomfort of pain, fire and brimstone. I'd be harder on myself than someone who loved me—loved me unconditionally—like the Great I Am would be.

I need fresh air. I rise in slow motion so I won't disturb my roommates. Janice's curled up in a ball on the air mattress, the tan blanket tangled around her body. Moving as slowly as possible, I grab my clothes and sneak into the bathroom. Once dressed, I drop my nightgown on my suitcase and quietly fish for my camera. My roommates' slow, even breathing and occasional soft snores assure me that I haven't disturbed them.

I step outside. It's brisk, but not too cold. This motel, located higher on the hill and about a mile off the highway, is a bit too far off the beaten track for me to head for downtown. It'd take too long and the others would wonder where I got off to. So, I explore the surrounding neighborhood.

Although the graying clapboard houses sit in various states of decay, the morning's golden glow makes everything look more authentic, richer. I snap a few photos of these old shacks and wander by a 1900s vintage passenger rail car that looks as if someone lives there as well. It must've been leaking: a blue plastic tarp weighted-down with tires drapes over part of its roof.

I return to the motel and listen at the door. It's silent. Everyone must still be sleeping. I sit down in the white molded plastic chair outside our room.

Moments later, Jeff emerges from KTVN's room.

"You're up early," he says a bit hoarsely. "I'm gonna grab some breakfast. Wanna join me?"

"Yes. I'm sick of protein bars."

He unlocks the vehicle's passenger door for me. "No telling how long the gas station stays open for breakfast. I thought it best to get there before they stop serving."

I nod. My eyes burn. I step into the vehicle and he gently shuts the door after me.

He slides behind the wheel, turns the key. "Wild night, huh?"

"To say the least. I don't think I'd believe it, if I hadn't gone through it."

We park on the side street next to the red building with a Western false front—like the ones they have on movie sets.

Once inside, we stand near the glass deli counter. I order an omelet, hash browns and tea.

"Why, hello there." Virginia waves to us from one of the picnic tables.

"Hi," we say almost in unison.

She scoots down a bit on the redwood bench. "I'm almost finished, but why don't you come join me?" She smiles so warmly, its authenticity shines in her blue eyes.

I walk over there, while Jeff selects a juice from the clear-paneled refrigerator unit.

"How did it go?" she asks. I can tell she got a good night's sleep. Her eyes are wide. Her voice clear and strong. I note she's wearing her generation's casual uniform of polyester pants and a paisley button-up shirt.

Jeff and I tell her the highlights. I realize then Jeff had been cheated. He had to experience everything through the camera. Worry about the focus. The lighting. Shot composition. Capturing the mood and action. He was so busy working the camera in manual mode, he experienced everything second hand.

Jeff excuses himself and goes to the men's room, leaving Virginia and me alone. The other table empties.

"It's great you visit Elizabeth regularly," I say.

Virginia scrapes up the last of her eggs with a wheat toast corner. "She gets lonely and I check on her. That's all."

"Well, she's lucky to have someone who cares about her." I take a sip of tea. "Honestly, I find your relationship with her quite touching."

She stops mid-chew, looking up at me with a confused expression. She shakes her head slightly and swallows. "I've got a busy day. I've got to go. Tell Bill to drop the key off before ya'll leave town. Have a safe trip back." She stands up, waves goodbye to Jeff as he emerges from the bathroom.

Virginia's coffee cup is two-thirds full. The door shuts behind her, sending silver bells jingling from its knob.

Hours later, our group meets a historian in Tonopah who escorts us to the old World War II airbase east of town. But while I'm physically present, my mind mires in nothingness, my muscles burn and my body drags with exhaustion. I wander the old wooden hangars, their loose rafters swaying in the breeze. These huge structures once housed the largest of bombers; today, they're home to barn owls. I walk the rocky soil, enjoying the solitude. Strangely enough, although I'm exhausted, my disease hasn't flared. Neither my pain nor my strength is any worse than the day before.

The following day, I eat lunch with the KTVN guys at the Fallon McDonald's before we hit the last stretch of desert roadway for home. Unlike Janice, Ted and Cheryl—who left at dawn so Ted could get to work on time—the four of us slept in and headed to Reno after shooting some promotional spots.

I chomp on a regular burger and small fries with extra salt. "Hey, did you get a chance to review the footage of the fourth floor footsteps?" I ask Jeff.

He nods. "Yeah. Last night." He takes a bite of his burger.

"Did you get it? The footsteps?" I ask.

Jeff shakes his head and swallows. "Nothing. Except for your uncontrolled scream." He fakes a look of horror. Kevin and Bill laugh.

I enjoy the ribbing. In just two days, this group has gone from being strangers to friends. I guess spending the night in a haunted hotel brings people together.

Bill's smile fades as he sets down his drink. "Really, nothing? Those were some of the heaviest, fastest footsteps I've ever heard."

My heart stops. Bill described the steps in exactly the same words I'd internalized. It occurs to me we never discussed what either of us experienced. He'd heard it the same way I did.

"It should've been there," Jeff says. "Maybe I'll be able to pull it out with the studio equipment."

He wasn't able to. The footfalls never recorded.

~19~
Home

I recount the trip's highlights as Ken and I sit at the dining room table drinking white zin. He leans forward and listens to my experiences, many of which he's heard before during our long distance phone conversations. I glance out the sliding glass window toward the setting sun and the dozens of quail grazing our newly sprouted yard.

"I wish I could've gone. I can't imagine experiencing those things," Ken says. "Who could've guessed?"

"I wish you were there, too. It blew me away." I take a sip of the chilled wine and gently twirl the glass by the stem. "Do you believe me? Do you believe these things really happened?"

Ken strokes his short copper beard with his thumb and index finger. "Honestly, I can't wrap myself around all of it. I'd have to go through it—as you did—to believe it. But, with that said, I do believe this experience was an important one for you." He takes my hand, squeezes, and then releases it.

Ken, ever analytical, earned his geology degree and later returned to school to get an MBA. He's a scientist at heart; even when I assist him with his volunteer work for Cornell University's Project Feederwatch, he insists on scientific accuracy for the data we submit. We record temperatures to a tenth of a degree, even though the online form asks for a temperature range. And he makes sure all bird counts are verified a second time before they're logged.

While I wish he'd look at me enthusiastically and say, "Yes. I believe it all happened," I know that isn't him. But he believes in me. After all, I know for a fact I wouldn't believe what happened in Goldfield if I hadn't gone through it. I appreciate his frankness and the fact he doesn't think I've lost my mind.

"Is there any way the voices could've been planted? Saved on the recorder earlier and played back?" he asks.

"You know, I didn't believe in EVP before Goldfield. I watched them record, rewind, erase and record again. But I did notice the basement recording had Cheryl's cough—which I remember her coughing—and I saw how wired they were when we got back to the motel. They just wouldn't shut up about the EVP. And if they did fake the recording, why would Cheryl cough? I really believe there were two spirits in there with us."

"Could you make out what the ghosts said without the investigators telling you what they said?" Ken's eyes mirror the forest green of his button front shirt.

"Yes. It was…amazing. I'd heard them play back the recorders all night. They'd think something was on there, but all I'd hear for the most part was white noise. But when they played it back in the basement, I easily made out the words. And so did Bill."

Ken drinks the last little bit of wine in his glass. "That's really something. Well, I'm glad to have you home and I'm happy it wasn't boring. How're you feeling? You seem to be doing all right."

The sun drops behind the desert foothills. The puffy clouds on the horizon turn a light orange.

"I'm exhausted. Foggy. And I can't wait to sleep in my own bed. Hmm." I watch the clouds spread, merge and change shapes in the darkening sky. "You know, you're right. I'm not doing badly. I'm tired, but who wouldn't be after what I did? In fact, I don't feel a bit worse. I feel the same as I did the day before I left."

"That's odd, but great." Ken stands up and kisses me. "Want another glass?"

"No, I'm fine. I wonder why I'm not worse. I should be stuck in bed with a helluva lot of pain. Maybe it's just going to take a little more time for all the adrenaline to get out of my system."

◆　　◆　　◆

Two days later, I remain mired in the same dense mental fog I've been in since Goldfield. I can't think straight or process anything. It's as if my brain's set on overwhelm. And the strange thing is these cognitive challenges are much different from the thinking problems I normally have due to my Chronic Fatigue Syndrome. I can come up with words. I can follow my thought streams. This time, the difference is Goldfield crowds out all my other thoughts. I can't focus on the news or even *The Simpsons*. My brain plays the 24-hour a day Goldfield Channel and nothing else. It runs repeatedly like it's in a video loop.

I sit in the sun on the dining room floor with my computer on my lap. My hope is to record everything about Goldfield so my mind will loosen its obsession. Out the sliding glass door, Ken digs up part of the drip system in his shredded Levis.

I pop up the laptop screen and turn it on. I need to preserve my memories before I start doubting them myself. The thoughts gush from my mind, flowing into my fingers. While I'm a fast typist, I still can't keep up with my brain, so I record only incomplete sentences, so I don't miss anything important. But while describing what I physically experienced, I realize I'm strangely detached, unable to crack open my numbness and delve into the chaotic emotions residing in me. It's as though my logical, rational side can't accept what I know happened. I stop a moment to rest my fingers.

A breeze blows the tail of Ken's plaid shirt, which has come untucked because of his digging. A scrub jay paces back and forth on the fence near him. Ken pulls a peanut in shell from his pocket, and throws it to the bright blue bird.

I wish Ken could've gone to Goldfield. We've shared everything these past 26 years. I'm sad there's nothing I can do to help him grasp, really understand, what happened. I know how outlandish I sound. Outside of Ken and my parents, I won't tell anyone else everything that occurred.

And there's the surprising issue of my still okay health. The inevitable chronic fatigue attack hasn't materialized. I should've been condemned to bed, wracked in pain and as limp as overcooked pasta, but my level of energy is like any other weekend. Not great. But also not as bad as it should be. My head hurts, but doesn't pound, and my joints and muscles aren't in any worse pain than they were before I left. *Why would that be?* Any stress, standing up and lack of sleep always condemn me to bed. Why would this time be so different?

But I'm thankful it is. And pray it stays that way.

~20~
Mind Movie

My friend Charlotte *(not her real identity)* and I order soup and salad at a coffee shop close to my office. We've been friends for a year or so and she wants to be among the first to hear about Goldfield. As the waitress removes our menus, she jumps right in.

"Tell me what you saw in Goldfield," she says. "I can't wait to hear about it." She leans toward me, her brown eyes peeking out from disheveled bangs.

"It was amazing. I felt emotions, heard voices, got touched—"

Charlotte shakes her head. "That's not what I meant. Tell me what you *saw*."

Gee, everyone else has been amazed. Anastasia said I'd give her nightmares. And here I am about to disappoint someone with my mind-blowing experience. I take my paper napkin, spreading it on my lap. "Well, I really didn't see anything. I saw some moving black mass float through the lobby, but besides—"

"Kathy." She sets her palms down on the glass-topped table, her neatly manicured pink nails perfectly shaped. "You *saw* a lot of things."

Her certainty disarms me. "What? Aw, come on." I don't know how to respond, so I laugh. "Yeah. I saw lots of little Caspers running around the halls. They said to tell you hi!"

She doesn't smile. In a very calm, even voice she says, "Trust me. You saw things; you're just blocking the images."

"No, I didn't!" My voice rises higher than I would've liked. I stop, take a deep breath and calm myself. I look about me. Luckily, no one from the tables around us seems to notice. "Why are you so convinced I saw something?"

Her eyes drop to her napkin. "There's something you don't know about me. I'm sorry—I just didn't think you'd understand. But now you will. Now you won't judge me. Don't get me wrong, I tell hardly anyone." She looks at me.

The table next to us erupts in laughter. A lead weight forms in my stomach.

"I can see what's in your mind, what you saw in Goldfield." She looks at me with a serious expression. "It's like a movie for me. And Kathy, you saw a lot."

My stomach grows heavier.

This has got to be a weird, twisted joke. Is she waiting for me to bite and then say "gotcha?" I've never known Charlotte to be that way. She's one of those bluntly honest, direct people. I always know where I stand with her. "What are you trying to tell me?" I say as the waitress places our salads in front of us. "Thank you," I say to the server.

Charlotte waits for the woman to leave. "I've always been this way. It's just something I keep to myself."

It finally dawns on me what she means. "You're telepathic?"

She nods and takes a bite of tomato.

Haven't I been through enough weirdness this past week? I try not to show my emotions, since she's confiding in me. And, it's evident she believes she's a telepath. What am I supposed to say to her? Even if she were, which I doubt, wouldn't I know if I saw something? I paste a pleasant grin on my face. "Perhaps you got your wires crossed? I know I didn't see anything, other than the black blob."

She shakes her head the whole time I'm talking. "Okay. The only way you'll believe me is if I tell you something. I normally don't do this, but I'll share one thing, just to show you I'm right and that you did see things." She pauses. "Remember when you first walked into the hotel? It was daytime and some man tripped near the front desk."

How would she know that? It was so insignificant, I didn't tell anyone about it.

"Yeah. I remember," I say warily.

"Why did he stumble?" she asks and takes another bite of salad.

"I guess he tripped over his feet. Nothing was there. Why?" I tear at a dried-out cuticle.

She giggles. "He tripped over a ghost dog. You saw a hound lying on the floor and you saw the man trip over it."

"Yeah. Ha ha. Good one!" She's pulling my leg. Though, I don't know how she'd know about the stumble. "Do you happen to know Janice or Cheryl?"

"Who are they? I only know you." Her expression looks a bit sad, disappointed. She stabs a carrot slice.

I soften my voice. "Then how do you know about this? The guy tripping?"

"I told you. I see the movies in your mind. You saw the guy trip over the hound."

"So, then, there are ghost dogs?" I start to get dizzy. What a weird anecdote. I push aside my salad. It's clear I'm not going to be up for eating.

"All animals have spirits." She pauses, looks at me with concern. "It's okay, Kathy. You did really well at Goldfield. You saw a lot of things and that's really good!"

I pull on the cuticle until it breaks off. "A lot of things?" My index finger bleeds. How could I see things and not know I had? How can she see what I don't remember? *I didn't know real people could be telepathic.* I study her face. She looks back at me with soft, compassionate eyes.

"Okay then, what else did I see?" I squeeze my hands together on my lap. Blood trickles down my finger and onto the white paper napkin, red spreading over the nothingness.

"This is something you need to work on. There's a reason you won't let yourself see the apparitions. I wanted you to know you did, so you can start to accept your abilities."

Work on this? I'm still not sure I believe her. Is there any other way she could've known about the man tripping? Even if she did know Janice or Cheryl, why would they mention it to her? Then I feel bad. Charlotte's always been honest with me, and I'm acting as if she's trying to put one over on me. What would be the point of her playing a charade such as this?

Heard it through the Grapevine plays in the background. Marvin Gaye's singing is almost as loud as the voices bouncing around the restaurant. Charlotte sips her cola and looks about her.

Okay. Let's suppose I've seen something and Charlotte can see inside my mind.

I need to know what I saw, so I can figure out why I'm repressing it. But I don't see a ghost dog now that she's told me. I don't see the man tripping over anything. I'm even irritated I can't remember who tripped…was it Kevin? Bill? Ted? I know it wasn't Jeff as he was filming. What other things did I see? And do I want to know? "Did I see something bad? Something frightening?"

She's quiet a moment as she seems to focus intently on me. "I don't think you saw anything scary."

"Thanks. Can you tell me a few other things?"

"You really need to unlock these images yourself." She takes another bite.

I want to reach across the table and shake her. Partly out of disbelief, partly out of fear. I wonder if my brain's trying to protect me, to help me hold on to a vestige of sanity.

"Is your salad okay?" the waitress asks me.

"It's fine. Thank you."

I sink back into the chair and grab the metal band on the sides. I guess I want to know. Maybe this explains the fogginess that won't dissipate. Perhaps I need to hear this to get back to normal. No. Things will never get back to normal. I'm living in a different world than I did before Goldfield. All the rules have changed. "Is this why my brain feels overloaded?"

"Probably. With time, you'll learn how to process everything you experience."

"Will you walk through the Goldfield with me right now?" I need to clear my mind; it needs to function. "Please, help me. At least with a few more things?"

"Okay, but I'm not going to tell you everything. Just some of the bigger stuff. I'm not sure it's best for you, but maybe if you learn you can see things, then your mind will open up more quickly. Here's one. Remember when you went down the basement steps, and you took that first right turn into the hall?"

"Yes."

"Two men stood near the entrance to the first room you entered. The room with the well."

"Okay." I take a deep breath. "What did they look like?"

"I'm not giving you all the information, as you really need to work on this. You can see them, if you just allow yourself to."

I concentrate on the dark concrete basement. The entrance to the water well room. I remember being scared, as this was right after Cheryl saw The Cowboy. Darkness. Cement. The stairwell. Nothing. "I can't see them."

"You will eventually. Okay, let's try this a little differently. Tell me about the little boy." "Cheryl saw him. I didn't—" I stop myself. She knows about the little boy, so she must

see him in my mind. I'm queasy. I don't like the idea that someone can see things I experienced and I can't.

"Now, Kathy," she says in her best mothering voice, "tell me about the little boy you saw on the fourth floor, just after you reached the landing."

"I can't see anything. Cheryl heard him. Cheryl went looking for him."

"But you're the one who found him. Look into yourself. How old was he?"

A group of diners pass by. It's getting crowded. I shift in my seat, then grasp the sides of the chair with force. I want to twist it. I search my mind, yet I can't see a damned thing. *Why the hell is this happening to me?* "I don't know, Charlotte. I CAN'T see him."

"He's a toddler, maybe four years old. Tell me what he was wearing."

"I don't know."

"Concentrate. Close your eyes. Accept you saw him. Focus on him. I'll give you a hint. He's wearing what he was buried in."

Wonderful. "Umm…. Before I do this—can you tell me if he looks dead? I can't handle looking at a dead child."

"No. He looks like a little boy," she says soothingly. "It's okay. Tell me what he wore."

I'm relieved to hear he doesn't look dead. Is Charlotte really telepathic? Am I really having this weird conversation with her? If this is in my brain, I can't think of any logical explanation for how Charlotte knows this. And I certainly don't want ghastly images of the dead floating around just waiting to pop out and scare me. I close my eyes. I picture the dilapidated fourth floor. Then a color comes to me. "A brown suit?" I'm not sure if I'm pulling this out of the air or not.

"Good. Yes. Describe it."

"I can't. It was a lucky guess."

"Kathy, if I can see it, so can you."

I want to run away. *Why am I being interrogated?* "I can't do this, Charlotte." *This can't be happening.*

"He was wearing those short pants—the kind kids wore a long time ago. Can you see him?"

The waitress sets down two steaming bowls of soup and leaves without a word.

"No. I can't. What's wrong with me?" My voice is weak.

"Nothing. It'll come with time. Just know you can see. One day when you're ready to accept seeing spirits, you'll be able to."

I think of the ghost who stroked my hair....Why do I think it's a woman? *God, maybe she's right.* My brain may be feeding me information in baby bites. "Charlotte, can you see who patted my head?"

She sets her spoon down and pushes her mousy brown hair behind her ear. "Now, Kathy. I wouldn't describe it as your head being patted. It's more like she was stroking your hair, feeling it."

I'm in the Twilight Zone. She knows everything in my brain. I hadn't told anyone the ghost stroked my head; I had used the word "patted" with everyone. Except for Ken. Because stroking just sounded too weird. So even if Charlotte knew someone else who went to Goldfield, there's no way for her to know this except for telepathy.

I wonder if I ever told her one of those polite lies, you know the kind you say to not hurt someone's feelings...but I stop this line of thought, as it isn't helping me now. "Okay, smarty pants. Yes. You're right. But did you see her?"

She chuckles. "You mean did YOU see her? Yes."

"Well, what did she look like?"

She shakes her head. "You need to work on this yourself. I've already told you way too much."

I lean toward her. "Please. Stop torturing me. Let me know. I won't ask about anything else. Was it Elizabeth?"

"You don't know her name. She wore a longish white dress. She had long blonde hair. I'd estimate she's around 17, but I'm not good at guessing adult ages."

"It could be her."

Billy, the carpenter, had described Elizabeth's ghost as having long blonde hair, teenaged, wearing a white dress. Part of me is excited; I want to climb a mountain and say, "Look at me! Look at the things I can see!" But just as strong a part, screams, "Oh my God! I don't want to see these things!" There's a whole world out here I didn't know existed or one I thought was only populated by odd people. Not normal people and certainly not me. If I can see the dead, I must be psychic. Why do I keep fighting this? Janice, Jason and Vickie said I was psychic. I've had unexplained experiences. I'm fighting this because I don't want to be a paranormal freak. I want to be normal. And this is not the way to do it.

"Would you like anything else?" the waitress asks.

Yes! A sane world. "Can I get this to go, please?"

"Certainly." She takes my lunch and leaves.

"Are you going to be all right?" Charlotte asks.

"I don't know. Too much has happened in the last week. Everything defies logic." My eyes well with tears. I fight to hold them back. "I'm never going to be normal, am I?"

"Depends on what you consider normal." She takes my hand and squeezes it. "You'll be fine. There's a reason this is happening to you right now. And I meant it when I said this is a good thing."

We walk out the door and hug goodbye. I get into my car, lock the door and...do nothing. I lean back into the fabric seat and let the sun's warmth permeate my body. I need to get back to work. I've already been away too long. But I don't start the engine. I can't take any more weirdness. Why is this happening to me? Why won't my mind let me see these images?

The answer comes to me quickly. Terror. Fear for my sanity. Fear of being judged. Being viewed as harshly as I have judged others. What will my Born Again friends think? Probably that I'm destined for hell. After all, that's what I would've thought a few years back. And what about my analytical, science-minded friends? They'll see me as a big joke: an irrational person living in a La La Land that only someone irreparably abnormal could believe in.

But it's the unknown that unsettles me most. Will I see things all the time now? When I'm in the shower? Or in the middle of the night—will the shadow people come back? Will I have any privacy?

And what am I supposed to do with this sixth sense? What if I see death? I won't be able to handle it. What if a spirit comes to me for help? I can't communicate with them. I can't send them to the light. I have no idea what I'm doing.

"God, why are you doing this to me?" I slam my fist down on my car's center console.

"What am I supposed to do with this ability? Where will the insanity end?"

Tears stream down my cheeks. *Who am I?* After I got sick, I learned I was not my career: I was my thoughts, my beliefs, my actions. But now my thoughts aren't my own and my beliefs have been turned upside down.

~*21*~
God's Answer

"She could see everything in my brain," I say to Ken as I lie on the couch with *O Magazine* open on my lap. I'm weak and exhausted. My joints ache and my skin burns.

Ken's at the dinner table, sorting through bills. "I wouldn't put much weight on what she said. There's really no substance to it." His voice is monotone.

"No substance? How can you say that?" I close the magazine and stiffly sit up, my joints fighting me every inch of the way.

Ken stares at the paperwork. "Well, maybe she knew someone in your group. They could've told her things and she parrots them back to you. Or maybe she's been there before and knew the layout of the place. I wouldn't get worked up over this if I were you."

Worked up? He's pushing my button—anger rises in my chest, prickly, constricting. I hoist myself off the couch; the magazine drops to the floor. I hobble over to him. "This is big! She doesn't know anyone else in our group. But for the sake of discussion—if she did befriend someone, why would that person tell her someone tripped next to the front desk? I didn't tell anyone about it, because it wasn't special." I try to catch his eye, but it doesn't work. He's intent on his bills. "And how in the hell would she know my head didn't get patted and instead was stroked? I didn't describe my head as stroked to anyone but you—even though that's what it was."

He finishes sorting his credit card receipts and picks up one pile. "Okay. I guess. I've got to get these paid tonight, okay?" He looks at me with tired eyes as he heads to our den/office.

He doesn't believe me. What did I expect? One week ago, no one could have convinced me of any of this. Why should I expect him to be any different? *Calm down.*

Cheryl told me it took years for her brother to believe her. Then he only did when something ghostly happened to him. I can't expect Ken to make the leap I have, because he hasn't gone through the paranormal three-ring circus I'm still stuck inside.

Gravity yanks at my body, threatening to pull me to the floor, so I go back and drop down onto the couch. My heart sinks. Ken's always been there for me. My best friend for 27 years. Who, upon seeing me stuck in bed for years, borrowed his father's trailer and drove me to Alaska to get me out of the house and lift my spirits. Who always found me pretty, even after I gained 80 pounds from being bedridden. And when the Mayo Clinic told me to accept that my health wouldn't improve, he rallied around me and insisted I keep trying new treatments, new doctors.

Why do I want him to fall off the same cliff I'm dangling from? I'm alone in this. For now. And I can't take the chance he'd stop loving me after all this. Of Ken thinking I've lost my grip on reality. Have I? My tales sound far-fetched to me and I'm living them.

I decide to censor myself around him. If it sounds too weird to me and I can't prove it, I won't tell him.

I lie in bed listening to the crickets' waning songs, dreading sleep for I fear what'll happen tomorrow. I just can't take much more. I can't.

Unfortunately for me, God seems to think I can handle more.

The house creaks. Not randomly, but in succession. It begins in the great room at the opposite end of the house. Moving almost rhythmically, like a person sauntering, to the start of the hall.

This house has always been noisy: it isn't well insulated. But I've never heard the creaks move in such a regular fashion and along a direct path—a course leading to my room.

It continues in the same rhythm further down the hall. Past Ken's room. At the bathroom. Past it. Toward my bedroom. The creaks mirror the same sounds as when someone walks down the hall. I pull the sheet over my head. I think of calling out to Ken. But I don't.

Please let this be my imagination. But after all that's happened, I can't blame my mind and just forget it.

Surely, ghosts can't follow people home, can they? What else could this be? I've never heard creaking like this.

Without looking toward the doorway, I slide open the bedside table drawer. Pull out my Bible, cradle it in my arms. Repeatedly, I recite the Lord's Prayer, drowning out everything but the sound of my voice under the covers.

It's Friday, nine days after Goldfield.

My muscles move more freely this morning. I get through my shower without having to rest afterward. My pain is less pronounced—enough so, I might be able to find a few minutes where my constant discomfort doesn't consume me. I'm better than I've been in months. Goldfield never caused an exacerbation. No weeks wracked in constant head-to-toe pain. Nor consecutive days of debilitating weakness, leaving me confined to bed. And that baffles me.

Perhaps Ken and I can do something fun this weekend, instead of me being consigned to the couch or bed.

The Goo Goo Dolls' "Iris" plays on the clock radio. The lead singer croons about people not understanding him.

There's one black pump next to the unmade bed. And I'm late. I have a meeting in 30 minutes and, if traffic is on my side, it will take 30 minutes to drive to the office. "Where is my dang shoe?" I drop to my hands and panty-hosed knees to look under the bed, swishing my hand where I can't gaze.

I hop up and search through the back corner of the walk-in closet. "I have to get out of here." I throw scrapbooking materials, sandals and dry cleaning into a pile outside my closet door. There. In the corner, I see the black pump. I must've kicked it off the last time I wore it, throwing it back where things never see light. I slip it on.

The traffic report airs on the radio. "We have an accident-free commute this morning…"

I do my last mirror check of the morning. Agh! Jewelry. This scoop-necked tank needs accessorizing. I open the mirrored jewelry case on the wall, grab the antique jade-heart necklace that Uncle George gave me.

"OOOH! Preeeetttty." It's a teenage girl's high-pitched voice. Crystal clear. Loud. As if someone's standing beside me.

I swing to my left, where I heard it. Nothing—no one—is there.

"I have to go!" I say aloud as I snatch the necklace off the hook and clench it in my fist.

The radio plays "Free Fallin'" by Tom Petty. I leave it on as I run through the laundry room, grab my bag and escape.

I'm losing my mind. This must be what insanity feels like. Hearing a voice when no one's there. But if I was really losing my mind, would I realize it? I speed out of the driveway, not waiting for the garage door to finish closing.

Perhaps a ghost did follow me home. But why would it? Was today's voice the same spirit creaking through our house? *Oh, God, what if there is more than one ghost in our home?* I drive down the Pyramid Highway, shaking my head. The jade heart lying in my lap. Is this what schizophrenia's like? She sounded real. Like she stood right next to me.

When is all of this going to end?

Once my meeting is over, I close my office door and call the natural foods store where Cheryl works. The phone rings once. Twice. My heart beats faster as I recheck the number on the phone display. Three times. "Please be there," I say to the ring tone.

"Hello. Herbal Haven." It's Cheryl.

I take a breath. "Hi. It's Kathy. Do you have a minute?"

"Sure. What's wrong?"

"I'm...I'm losing my mind." I push a swath of papers off the center of my desk and set my head down upon my arm on the cleared space. "I think a ghost followed me home from Goldfield. I heard...It was a teenager's voice. She complimented my necklace. She said it was pretty." It seemed odd to me that something immaterial—a ghost—should like something material such as a piece of jewelry. "What's going on with me? Have I lost my mind?"

"No. You're fine, Kathy. It's okay," she says sympathetically. "Goldfield opened your third eye. It's made you more open to psychic experiences."

"I don't know if I want this happening."

"It's a good thing to know who's around you. Spirits are everywhere, you know."

"I don't want things watching me. I like having alone time. What if something shows up and I'm in the shower? I don't know. I just don't know if I can handle this." I sit up and roll a ballpoint pen around the top of my desk.

"It's okay. Remember, you are in control. You tell them what you want. If you don't want them in the house, then ask them politely to leave. But don't worry. You're not crazy. You'll get used to it."

I can't fathom getting used to it. To having ghosts around me. Talking to me. Watching me.

I'm brushing my teeth when Ken—smelling of soap and mint Crest—walks up behind me. He looks in the mirror. Puts his hands on my waist.

I stop brushing my teeth. "You ready for bed?"

He nods. "I wanted to talk to you about something." He's smiling impishly, so I know he's ready to tease me. "Ever since you got home last week—" He says in his best Dracula voice. "I've been hearing noises. I think you've brought home a ghost. BOOOOOOOH!" He laughs, but something about his expression—an edge of seriousness—makes me wonder if he thinks it's true.

I go rigid, but try to hide my reaction by resuming brushing my teeth. I roll my eyes at him to buy time.

Did he hear the footsteps the other night? I want to ask, but I don't want to chance it in case he really is teasing. I spit and rinse, wiping my mouth off with the hand towel. I'm hoping he'll move on to another subject. But he doesn't. He just watches me.

So I speak up, "That's ridiculous! Ghosts don't follow people home." I try to keep my voice calm.

"Okay, little ghost hunter." He squeezes my waist and goes back to his room.

I look in the mirror. I'm not the person I was just a week and a half ago when I prepared to go to Goldfield. I'm completely different, even though I look the same. It's just that I've lost what it feels like to be Kathy Berry. Can Ken tell?

I slip under the covers. The Bible lies atop the bedside table within arm's reach. With some trepidation, I turn off the light. Within minutes, the creaks start up again at the far end of the house. I can't keep doing this. Enduring the unknown. I should take control, but terror paralyzes me. The sound travels steadily down the hall, moving ever closer to the bedroom. "Ken," I call out, "Are you asleep?"

No answer.

It pauses near the pantry entry, just a few feet from my doorway.

Coyotes yip in the distance. It's a sound that normally relaxes me, but tonight their ethereal howling further puts me on edge. The noise arrives. It's at my door.

I grab my Bible, turn over on my stomach and pull the covers over my head and say an urgent prayer. "Oh Lord, please help me. I am losing my mind. I can't handle this. It's too much. Please."

It creaks just inside my room. I tighten my grasp on the Bible. "Please God, stop all of this. Please protect me. Look after me. Ohh, make these noises stop." I'm crying. Shaking. My hands hurt from clasping the Good Book so tightly. I'm so done. I want my normal life back. "Please help me." The creak is at the foot of my bed. I dare not look up. I just know deep down I wouldn't be able to handle what I'd see. Out of desperation, I say to the Great I Am in a harsh tone, "I'm trying so hard. You've put me through so much lately, and you aren't looking after me!"

Inside my head, a booming male voice scolds me. "Of course I am looking out for you." He speaks like an angry father talking to an ungrateful child: *me.* He's so loud, his voice vibrates inside my brain.

Oh no! I didn't expect an answer. I guess I thought the Lord wouldn't listen to me. I brace for His wrath and shut my eyes tight against the pillow. *What have I done?* I'd rather face a creaky ghost than to tick off God.

"I'm sorry. I didn't mean to be insolent. It's just…I'm at the end…I can't take any more. It's too much." I think of all the smiting he did in the Old Testament. Every muscle tenses. My crying intensifies.

"I've looked out for you every minute of your life. Especially now." The forceful voice still scolds but it's a bit softer. "Why do you think I put the people around you that I did? Janice, Cheryl, Vickie, Charlotte. Don't you think it strange you know so many psychics? If you'd gone through this a few years ago, you'd have no one to help you through it.

"I look after you, as I look after others." His voice turns loving, compassionate. "I even made sure after Goldfield you would spend the night with others—I didn't want you alone. That's why I put the four of you in one little room."

He's forgiven my transgression! The Great I Am's forgiven my disbelief. My muscles ease.

Place and time have stopped. So have the creaks. It's just my Lord and me. I don't hear coyotes. I don't hear Ken rustle.

"No matter the trial you go through, I place people around you to help you get through the difficult times. That's *how* I take care of you."

Oh my dear God! I stop crying. I've always believed in the Almighty's omniscience, but I guess I never really grasped the Lord would be so intricately involved in the details of my life.

I turn over and brazenly stare at the ceiling. I'm no longer afraid. If God looks out for me by orchestrating the tiniest of my life's details, I can only imagine what else the Almighty's done for me. Perhaps all miracles are rooted in the small, seemingly insignificant moments in our lives. Small events—going unnoticed as we navigate our too busy worlds—are important enough to command God's attention. This realization calms and awes me, placing lightness throughout my being.

"Thank you. Thank you so much Lord. I love you. I had no idea. Please forgive me."

I think of the last 18 years, battling these blasted diseases. How God had taken care of me. I gained strength from those around me, those who never gave up: Ken, my parents, a friend who battled severe arthritis and could commiserate with my chronic pain, among others. How many times had I leaned on these people when I could no longer fight for myself?

I silence my brain, hoping the Great I Am will share more with me. But nothing comes through.

God must think I'm important enough to talk to. This sickly individual who's never done anything impressive. How little I feel I deserve this attention. Yet the Lord gave me this wondrous gift. If God feels I'm worthy, then I am.

I desire to capture this revelation—this powerful sense of love and being cared for—and encase it in stone. So I won't ever feel abandoned. Scared. Hopeless. Again.

As a child, God visited me. Regularly. But as I grew to be a logical adult, the sensations of divine closeness diminished, until the Lord stopped coming by completely. At least, that's what I'd thought.

Now, I realize the Almighty's always been alongside me. Looking out for my welfare. It's at once the most freeing and powerful feeling in the world.

Right then, another thought occurs to me. One just as wondrous as the Lord's personal concern for me. *God didn't smite me!* In being so insolent, so unappreciative, I should've been punished by the Almighty. The Great I Am should've abandoned me, telling me I was on my own. After all, I demonstrated a total lack of trust.

But that's not what the Lord did. The Almighty's response was unconditional love and enduring patience. No fire and brimstone. No vengeful rage. Nor smiting. God hadn't given up hope for me. The Lord's love is apparently too strong for that.

God answers my prayers in the love surrounding me: the Lord's pure, strong love along with the tenderness and caring of those divinely put on my path.

I turn on my side and my cheek hits my moist pillow.

How little faith I have. *I'm sorry, God. Sorry to have doubted you.* I pray I never do again.

With billions of people on this earth, the Lord orchestrated details down to who would spend the night in a room in the Santa Fe Motel! It's dizzyingly complicated to think how the Great I Am orchestrates the lives of billions of people. Why should I be afraid of a creaking house when God is right beside me?

I gently place my Bible back in the drawer. God is here. Protecting me. I don't need to use His Book for physical protection any more. The actual Great I Am watches over me!

My relationship with the Lord takes a huge leap forward. It dawns on me what a "personal relationship" with the Great I Am could really be. The Almighty treated me as an individual. Even spoke to me. Explained things. Shared wisdom. Tonight, God became more real, more tangible than I ever believed possible.

I clasp my hands in thankful prayer. "Oh, Lord, help me hear your whispers. Help me feel your nudges. Help me remember you're always here and that your love endures like no other. Help me be aware of the total love you bestow on me—this very common human being—and help me be worthy of it."

I curl up into a ball and fall into a rare, peaceful slumber.

~22~
Cal Neva Ghosts

The sun casts a golden path across Lake Tahoe's waters as we discuss our paranormal hunt strategy at the Cal Neva Resort in Crystal Bay, Nevada. I look across the expanse of turquoise, lapis and aqua waters to the powdered snow summit of Mt. Tallac, and think how odd to witness such exquisite beauty while discussing ghosts.

The six of us (Kevin's not joining us tonight) sit around the large circular table in the Lakeview Dining Room. The lights are low. White linen tablecloths. Fresh flowers. Couples holding hands. There's romance all around us as we lean in to the center of the table talking of nothing but the paranormal. The Cal Neva doesn't have a coffee shop, so clad in our jeans and khakis, we dine in this gourmet restaurant.

"It'd be good to have someone from the Cal Neva at the séance." Cheryl pushes her hair away from her face. Her nails are painted pumpkin orange. "The spirits might come out more if there's someone present they know." She grabs a breadstick from the basket and takes a bite.

"Good idea. Let's see about the general manager participating," Bill says. "I thought we could hold the séance around midnight, after we've visited Marilyn and Frank's cabins."

Bill's talking about Marilyn Monroe and Frank Sinatra. Once owned by Old Blue Eyes in the early 1960s, the Cal Neva had become the playground for the famously famous. Rumor has it the Rat Pack—Frank,

Dean Martin, Sammy Davis Jr., Peter Lawford and Joey Bishop—had held drunken parties, bordering on orgies here. Marilyn had been a frequent visitor, as was Juliette Prowse and mobster Sam Giancana. They'd traveled an extensive network of tunnels to each other's cabins, the showroom and the boathouse. Celebrities had played underground, while their fans had strolled the buildings above them.

The sun drops behind the Sierra. The changeling skies turn from a fiery orange to a rosy alpenglow. The waitress serves our food as the lake turns into a large, black void.

A man in a blue Cal Neva T-shirt bumps into the waitress as she turns to leave, yet he ignores her. "You're the TV people, right? The ones looking for ghosts? I need to speak with you." He looks as though years of cigarettes and liquor had taken a toll on him. Wrinkles frame his mouth. He's too thin, as is his hair. He smells musty. "Please don't tell them I talked to you."

Bill reaches his hand toward the man. "We'd love to hear your stories. I'm Bill Brown and this is—"

The man gives Bill one quick shake of his hand. "I don't have much time." His eyes flit back to the dining room entrance. "I heard you're going into the showroom tonight. Don't. Something's evil there."

"Sounds like you've had an experience," Bill says cheerfully.

I inwardly smile, as Bill loves ghost stories—even if it comes as a warning to us.

The man's eyes land on Bill only briefly before he scans the room again. "Yeah. I have stories. Something very bad is there. Don't mess with it. I just wanted you to know." He paces between Bill and me.

His darting eyes, his pacing and his rushed demeanor seem a little too theatrical for me. Could management have sent him to build a juicier story and generate more publicity for this resort that has fallen on tough times? After all, one of the first things the general manager told us was this resort was built on an ancient Indian burial ground. *Oh, please!*

"We'd love to hear what happened in the showroom. Let me get you a chair," Bill says.

"No thanks. I'll just say my piece. Then get back to work. My friend—he wasn't the same after he saw it. It was bad."

"What are you doing?" The portly general manager shatters the peace of the dining room with his reprimanding tone. The diners, who have stopped eating, stare at us. He rushes up to us. "I've asked you not to disturb our guests."

"Someone had to warn them. I'm—I'm sorry," the man mutters to the floor.

The GM's face is red. He shakes his finger. "You're still on the clock. You better get back to your job. That is, if you want to keep it."

Bill lifts his eyebrows.

The man leaves without another word. Bill calls after him, "Thank you for telling us."

The manager grasps his round stomach. "Sorry. He's an attention hound. Some people will say anything to get on TV. Let me assure you, no one else will disturb you tonight. Let me know if there's anything we can do for you."

Bill sets his water down. "If you have time, we'd love for you and perhaps one or two of your staff to join us for the investigation and a séance later tonight. Perhaps—"

"No. You don't want him. I'll help and get my assistant manager or Sheila in marketing. We can discuss this after your meal. Come by my office for the cabin keys when you're through dining. Enjoy!" He shuffles out of the restaurant.

"That was interesting," Bill says. "Janice, what do you think of that story?"

Janice, who's extensively researched the history and hauntings of the Cal Neva, shakes her head a bit warily. "I've never heard of or experienced anything evil here." She takes a drink of coffee and dabs her lips. "There is the Shaman, though. The employees talk about him."

"Well, we know this area was the summer grounds for the Washoe Indians." Bill says. "So I guess it could be a possibility." He takes a bite of salad.

"Management used to have a photo of the Shaman apparition. I've seen it. It's quite remarkable, even though it's grainy. They said the janitor took the photo with his cell phone. I'm sure the GM would show it to us if they still have it."

We stand in the GM's darkened office, a streetlight from the parking lot providing us little illumination. The assistant manager fumbles with the computer, opening various files, but not finding the Shaman. We crowd around the monitor.

"Why don't I turn on the light?" Janice offers.

"Nah. I know it's here. You'll be able to see the photo better in the dark. It's just a cell phone picture. I remember the night our maintenance guy saw this. He was shaken. I'd never seen him like that. Here." He clicks on a file, and a black and white photo pops onto the screen.

A shaggy white creature. Its face dark, featureless. A gauzy apparition. Its clothes flowing, tattered. You can almost see through him. I shiver. Then, I get irritated with myself. *It's probably a fake.* It's probably been PhotoShopped. I hope.

Marilyn Monroe's cabin at the Cal Neva Resort. Photo by Kathleen Berry.

We stand in front of Marilyn's beige cabin. The paint peels off the door and the trim.

There's a crisp breeze and in the momentary quiet of our group, I hear the lake's waves beat against the boulder-strewn shore. The sky's a silky black and the stars shine as diamonds. A fitting night to visit the haunt of the world's most glamorous movie star.

Jeff turns the camera light on. Bill unlocks the cabin door and speaks to the camera. "This was Marilyn Monroe's cabin, back in the Cal Neva's heyday. Let's see if she's still sticking around." He enters as Jeff takes sweeping footage of the tiny room, before the rest of us file in and fill it completely.

The interior is off-white. White wicker chairs. Wicker headboard. Thank goodness for the green floral bedspread and matching curtains, which add some color to this room. Black and white framed posters of Marilyn adorn the walls.

I sit on a chair in the corner, near the walk-in closet, to get out of the way.

"None of the furnishings today were here when Marilyn visited," the GM says while staring into the camera. "She had a heart-shaped bed and after she died, people would stay in this room and pull out a bit of the mattress as a souvenir. Since it became more suitable as a souvenir than a bed, we had to replace it." He sniffs loudly.

I sit underneath one of Marilyn's posters. It's a close-up. She's laughing; her head's thrown back as blonde curls escape the cowboy hat she's wearing. Seductively, her pinkie plays with her lower lip. I imagine she's given sweet dreams to many a man who's rented this room.

Janice, Ted and Cheryl enter the walk-in closet that looks bigger than the bathroom. "The tunnel came up through here," Janice says, pointing at the closet floor.

"Is it still under there?" Bill asks.

A pressure builds against my chest. A strange heaviness.

"No. The Feds destroyed them," the GM says. "After gaming officials found out Sam Giancana visited here, Sinatra lost his gaming license. So, under the guise of preventing interstate trafficking, they caved the tunnels in."

The pressure gets heavier on my chest. I have to take deeper breaths to get air.

"Recording," Ted says.

"Hi, this is Ted and we just wanted to talk with you. Marilyn, are you here?"

We all look around as if she would just materialize in front of our eyes. I admit it would be cool to have her appear and have her famous white dress billowing about her.

"Marilyn, they say you tried to commit suicide here. Did you try to take your own life?" He pauses. "Or did someone try to kill you?"

Whether it's area folklore or fact, it's said she attempted suicide by overdose in this very cabin only weeks before she successfully killed herself.

Ted's arm extends toward the middle of the room. He's wearing a large khaki T-shirt with sunglasses hanging around his neck. "Can you tell us who was with you that night?"

Janice motions to Ted, then she speaks up. "Were you happy here?" Pause. "Did you have a liaison here with Bobby Kennedy?" She motions to the rest of us to try the EVP. No one steps forward, so the paranormal investigators shut off their recorders. I see a flash of concern on her face when she looks at me.

I mouth "Okay," even though I don't feel that way. The heaviness bears down on my lungs. Could I be coming down with the flu?

"Let's see what we've got," Ted says as he looks at the counter on his voice-activated recorder. Janice and Cheryl crowd around him, comparing their numbers as well.

"Well, it doesn't look like I got anything—but Ted, Janice, your readouts are quite a bit longer," Cheryl observes.

I fidget as Janice and Ted play back their recorders against their ears.

"I've got something." Janice pushes Rewind, then Play. Ted's voice comes on. "…Did you try to take your own life?" He pauses.

"ONNOOOWN." I hear a garbled noise but can't quite make it out.

Bill nods. "Can we hear that again?"

"Certainly. I think she's saying 'on own'—that she killed herself." Janice presses Play.

"ONNOOOWN." I can just barely make out the words. But it isn't anywhere near as clear as Goldfield's Basement EVP. The weight on my chest intensifies. I attempt to take a deep breath, but only succeed at getting a shallow one.

"I've got something too," Ted says. "Here, listen." He holds out the recorder. It sounds like static. White noise. I can't make anything out except it leaves me with a chill.

"Good job, Teddy," Cheryl says. "She's saying 'help me'."

"Good stuff." Bill looks at his watch. "How 'bout we head to Frank's place?"

As soon as I step out of the cabin, my chest clears, my breathing eases and the heaviness lifts. No flu would resolve itself that quickly. Could I have been feeling Marilyn's desperation? Regardless, I'm relieved to be out of those cramped quarters. But I also wonder what kind of help the spirit needed and if we should've done something for it.

Frank Sinatra's cabin is not much bigger than Marilyn's. A wicker chaise lounge sits near the closet, and the posters here are of Old Blue Eyes.

"Hold on a second," Jeff says as he sorts through his camera pack. "I need a new battery. This one's running low."

Everyone talks among themselves. I crouch down and Jeff hands me the low battery. "This'll only take a minute," he says.

Clank!

"OOOOH!" most of the group exclaims.

"Did you see that?" Janice's voice is higher than usual.

"The remote. It just levitated!" The young assistant manager's eyes are large.

Bill looks around the room. "Kathy, Jeff, did you see it?"

We shake our heads.

Bill looks about the room…"how many of you saw this?"

Janice, the GM, the assistant manager, Ted and Cheryl raise their hands.

"It was the weirdest thing," Ted says. "One end lifted into the air and then slammed down on the dresser."

Bill picks up the remote, turning it over as he examines it. "Looks normal enough." He pushes the dresser. Nothing moves. "Could someone have accidently moved it?"

A chorus of "no" follows. "It moved on its own. It really did," Janice says as the other witnesses nod their heads in agreement.

Dang! I would've loved to see something levitate. Is there anything spirits can't do?

◆　　◆　　◆

160

I lounge in one of the lower showroom booths, resting. Jeff and I are the only ones here, everyone else is getting some refreshments.

The showroom is a relic of the 1960s, and in my opinion, the mod looks of that era were never attractive. Everything colored gold, olive, orange, brown. Huge, angular cutouts line the off-white walls: African dancers, a mandolin player, an Egyptian playing some flute-like instrument, and a large Polynesian mask among other gaudy art.

Cal Neva showroom. Photo by Kathleen Berry.

I stretch out my legs across the booth and lean back into the padding. My joints cry out with each movement and if it could, gravity would just suck me down into the depths of the earth. Jeff's in the back of the room setting up his tripod. All the doors, except for the main front entrance, are locked as the GM worries about pranksters disturbing the séance.

My eyes scan the stage, the big heavy curtain blocking off the back half of the performance arena. A round banquet table with seven chairs has been set up in the front half of the stage.

Then I see it. Darkness passes through the slit in the curtain panels. Black. Then light. Jeff and I are the only ones here, aren't we? I stare at the inches-wide gap at the center of the drapes. Perhaps my eyes are tricking me. Then it happens again. Light. Dark. Light. Movement. I jump out of the booth.

"Jeff, aren't we alone?"

He looks up from his gear. "Yes. No one else has come back. Why?"

"I'm going to get the GM. I think one of his employees snuck in and is behind the curtain."

As I get to the front door, the GM arrives with the rest of the team. After I share my observations, we fan out across the stage with all the lights on. No one's there and all the doors are locked. I think of that man saying evil's in here. Then of the Shaman. Neither option makes me comfortable. I say a prayer to God for protection, and feel confident I'm being watched over.

For the séance, everyone—except for Bill who is observing and Jeff who is manning the camera—sits around the white draped round banquet table that's set up on Frank's stage.

Nothing much comes out of the séance itself. It's Bill who contributes to the investigation. He saw something dark pass just beyond the curtains only feet away from us. A validation of my earlier experience.

I'm thinking we're just about done for the night when the GM speaks up.

"Are you up to investigating one more place? There's room 101. The staff doesn't like to go in, and some flat out refuse to enter it. You see, a while back—15 or so years ago—one of our employees killed himself there. You may find it an interesting place to visit."

Bill looks at us. "You guys want to do this? I realize it's a work night. But, I'm game if you are."

Suicide. My gut tightens. I don't know if my trepidation is due to my memory of contemplating stepping in front of a speeding semi years earlier, or if it's the grief residing in me from my uncle's suicide almost thirty years ago. I don't want to go in there. But, this is work; I have to be a team player.

Everyone else enthusiastically agrees to go. I stay silent.

"Kathy, are you up to it? It won't take long," Bill says.

"Let's do it." Cheryl nods my way.

I'm riding with KTVN, so I can't just leave on my own. And I don't want to hinder Bill's story. I muster a smile. "Let's do it."

"I've never been in there," Janice says. "I love investigating something new."

Room 101 looks like any other modern hotel room. The almost mandatory scenic watercolor. Floor-length drapes. Low dresser and large mirror. I stand at the back near the door with Bill, the GM and his assistant. Ted, Cheryl, Janice and Jeff are on the other side of the room conducting EVP.

It's Cheryl's turn to ask questions. "How did you kill yourself?"

I catch movement near Cheryl and see something that, at first, I think is the swag lamp, but it isn't. It's bigger and swinging from the ceiling near them. Legs dangling during death's throes. Without thinking, I turn to Bill and grasp my neck. "He hung himself," I say softly, surprising myself at my conviction.

Bill gives me a questioning look, then whispers. "How do you know? Did you hear about it?"

I shake my head. "I just know." I could see this man dying. *I saw him!* This realization startles me, filling me with fear and dread.

"Where did it happen?" Bill asks.

I point near the window. My eye catches movement again. In my mind, there's no one in this room except for a man looking out the window. He's desperately sad. Then I see the swinging again.

"But Kathy, there's nowhere for someone to hang himself."

The GM places his hand on Bill's arm. "She's right. He did it. There. By the window. The room was completely remodeled after it happened."

They both look at me. Grimly.

I place my hands on my forehead and shrink back into the far wall. I don't want to see death and dying. Oh Lord, please don't ever show me his strangled face.

~23~
Fear

The swaying legs remain foremost in my mind. Even days later. Bits of the mind movie focus ever clearer over time. His casual brown slacks. The body slowly turning, lifeless. The downturned head. But, thank God, no face.

I start to realize I've been spared. My trepidation at seeing his dull eyes and gaping mouth lessens with each passing hour. I tell myself, if I don't see his visage, he wasn't real and never lived. Right now, I'll convince myself of anything if I just don't have to deal with it.

I peel potatoes over the aluminum sink, staring out the window. Black, heavy clouds clump over the foothills, deadening the greens of our fall lawn. Perhaps we'll luck out and get rain tonight. I soak in this instant of normalcy. Of fixing dinner. Water bubbles on the stove and the aroma of honey-glazed turkey fills the kitchen. My back aches from bending over the sink, and my skin burns against my cotton blouse.

I set a stripped potato down on the produce bag and stare into the chaotic pile of peelings spread across the bottom of the sink. *It's only been about a month since Goldfield.* It feels like years. Ages since I lived in a safe, logical, understandable cocoon.

I remind myself that by breaking free of my cocoon's thin, yet confining walls, I've encountered great blessings. Amazing gifts. After all, if I hadn't gone to Goldfield, would God have talked to me? And if the Lord had, would I have heard it? And what of the pleasant spirits who interacted with me as well? The ghost who stroked my hair. The unseen specter who recorded his politely worded message on Cheryl's recorder. I can't turn my back on such wonders.

Then there are the multiple realms of my new reality. The human, earthly existence. The spirit world. Everything so complex. Something has to keep order. Someone intelligent beyond all to create such a complicated universe. God's grown larger to me, overseeing more than I could ever imagine while playing such integral, intimate roles in each of our lives.

Sprinkles splatter the concrete porch. The breeze through the slightly opened window kisses my kitchen-warmed cheeks and I inhale deeply. The refreshing scent of wet sagebrush wafts in from the hills a couple blocks away.

I used to think all ghosts were evil, satanic. But Goldfield's spirits treated us with civility and compassion, hardly what I'd expect from the devil. Even the Trinity includes the Holy Ghost. How did I ever get so off-balanced as to fear them all?

But fearing spirits isn't completely wrong. Evil exists. After all, the dark side proves its reality in our everyday world. Revealing itself in inhumanity. Cruelty. Horrific actions taken by people. Murderers. Torturers. Rapists. Since the soul lives on, these evil essences must also continue in some form.

Fortunately, God prepared me for my interactions with the spirit realm. Vickie taught me about invoking the prayer for protection. Cheryl told me about positivity attracting positive spirits and to treat the unseen with the same respect I would accord a human. How dangerous it would have been to jump into ghost hunting without knowing what to do, how to do it and how to protect myself.

My thoughts turn to the cable television ghost busters hurling insults and yelling at entities unseen. Their rudeness inviting negative elements to interact with them. The potential evil these TV personalities could stir up. They're playing with forces they'd be better off leaving alone.

If my circumstances had been different, I could've unknowingly provoked evil. And I've no doubt that experience wouldn't have been godly or affirming. This knowledge reinforces God's further importance in my life: the Lord is my shield, my bulletproof vest that when worn, protects me from harm.

I pull out the wooden cutting board and a sharp knife, and rinse the peeled potatoes. The warm water spills over my hands.

I can't fully grasp the complexity of the world I now accept. It's too wide open. Expansive. I miss the confines of the "comfortable, logical world." Of the black and white laws governing three dimensions and five senses. With this tether to the known severed, I'll either fly to amazing heights or crash down in a heap of insanity.

Will odd, eerie instances ever stop happening to me? And how can I find comfort in this new reality? For right now, I hate the unease, the uncertainty. Of waiting for the next experience to engulf me. I'm scared of seeing things, especially death. And I really don't want spirits to visit me in the night.

I chop the spuds, listening to the blade clomp rhythmically against the board.

The Bible teaches we all possess free will. So, it figures that once we die and rid ourselves of these bodies, our free will continues. Such vast opportunity intrigues me. To learn and grow. Freedom from fear.

That's it. I stop mid-chop. Fear holds me back. It had kept me from acknowledging the small, odd incidents, which happened over my life. Fear of the unknown. Trepidation about being different and being seen as a freak.

If I'd embraced those experiences, I'd have been better prepared to handle the past month. In Goldfield, I clung to terror like a security blanket. I bet I missed opportunities in my closed state I may never have again. What if I'd realized I had seen the little boy when he had appeared on the fourth floor? I could've spoke to him, learned about him.

Until this point, I know I've missed the signals, the signs of those who've passed and wanted to convey a message. Messages that could've brought me strength, love and a more intimate relationship with God earlier in my adult life. How my logical mind blocked out or explained away spirits' attempts to reach me all these years. And despite my scared attempts to deny the paranormal's existence, they kept trying to get my attention.

What an amazing testimony to heavenly love. God's love. For when the Almighty faced Kathy Berry's wall, the Lord didn't give up. Instead, the Great I Am disassembled my wall one brick at a time. A wall I built up based on other people's logic and the rationality of our society. Of the pulpit's condemnation of pursuing knowledge of the paranormal. Of church warnings that all psychics and psychic abilities come from Satan. Of science saying the world is only what we can see and that those who believe in the silliness of specters and such must be dim-witted.

Despite my wall, the Lord, angels and spirits continued to reach out to me, until eventually, the barricade crumbled and I opened up.

Fear insidiously had built a stranglehold through a series of small squeezes, easy enough to disregard until I was clenched in a vise created by this unstable emotion.

By listening to my inner frightened voices about rejection and losing face, I sometimes half-heartedly pursued the goals I wanted to achieve. If I didn't whole-heartedly put myself out there to reach my potential, then when I failed, I wouldn't risk knowing "I did everything in my power to achieve my dreams and I still fell short." I wrote three drafts of a novel, but it wasn't ready to send to agents. So I sat on it for years. Not my fault, though, because perhaps one day I'll finish it and send it out. Maybe it'll get published. Then I'll be successful.

What I failed to realize, though, was my inability to see my dream reach fruition meant I doomed myself before I wrote my novel's first word. Being too afraid to give my best condemned me to failure and prevented me from achieving my potential.

Fear limits me. And, those strangulating restrictions eventually extinguish hope.

The sprinkles cease and the breeze turns into a full-on wind, blowing the daily newspaper off the kitchen island. It floats suspended until the pages separate and it showers down to the floor. I shut the window and watch the trees sway. Then, I push the potatoes off the board into the pot of boiling water.

Fear infringes on other areas of my life as well. At times, it prevents me from reaching out to others, making myself vulnerable enough to forge strong, trusting relationships.

Angst keeps me closed-minded, as it's easier to feel safe in a smaller, more understandable world. And easier for me to control that sphere.

Never had I thought of myself as a scared person until now. I believed I'd lived a full life. After all, I've fought a debilitating illness for 18 years. Many couldn't do what I've done. In not facing their disease and their horrific imaginings for their futures, they killed themselves.

On a larger scale, it seems very possible fear causes much of the world's ills. It makes us judge and distrust others. Encourages us to place ourselves above everyone else, to give us a false sense of superiority. We look down on groups different from us. Richer. Poorer. They look different. They act different. They speak a language we don't understand.

Even the terror of poverty drives greed.

Fear causes sin! *Wow!*

Burdened raindrops beat against the shingles. The cloud's blackness falls to the ground, obscuring the hills.

Fear causes sin. How clear it is to me now.

As an adult, my consternation about the Old Testament's Vengeful God kept me at arm's distance from the Most Supreme Being, which was amazing, since as a child I had experienced such divine adoration. But as I matured, I focused so much on other things—being a logical grownup seeking career success and finding an ideal mate—that I'd taken the direction of my life away from the Almighty. But I'd behaved, so I thought that vengeful God would turn elsewhere to smite the bad and evil. Who wants a frightening, omnipotent being involved in every aspect of their lives?

My fear of God distanced me, leaving me unable to fully embrace the Lord's love and forge a deep personal relationship with the Great I Am.

Right now, in my kitchen with the potato water hissing, it seems to me trepidation is behind everything negative and limiting in my life.

That night, I open my Bible to 1 John 4:16 to 18, confirming the insights I had while preparing dinner.

> *"God is love....There is no fear in love. But perfect love drives out fear, because fear has to do with punishment. The one who fears is not made perfect in love."(NIV)*

God doesn't want my fear. The Most Supreme Being craves my love.

As I close the Bible and set it in the drawer, the fog that had bedded down in my brain since Goldfield, lifts.

I've finally gotten the message.

~24~
Controversy

Ted, Cheryl and Janice part ways. Their passions divide them now. Janice says the voices in the Goldfield's basement are hers, not electronic voice phenomena. Ted and Cheryl are convinced both are Class A EVPs and that the second one was a spirit's manipulation of Janice's words.

I'm conflicted. How could we have been so thoroughly convinced the voices were ghostly? And why would the investigators be so convinced that they talked of nothing else in the Santa Fe Motel?

I don't want to believe in something that isn't true. Especially since these EVPs had such an emotional and spiritual effect on me.

I find the raw footage of us in the hotel's subterranean barbershop. KTVN had given Ted a disk of this unedited filming. So they'd have indisputable proof of their claims. When I asked, Ted gave me a copy of it.

I lower myself down to the blue carpeting, grabbing the TV stand to balance myself, as my legs don't want to bend. I sit only inches from the television, a yellow legal pad of paper, pen and DVD remote in my lap. I'm determined to dissect the footage and write down every word spoken by us mortals, along with any ambient noise and compare it with the resulting EVP footage.

The KTVN menu comes up. I press Play.

We're in the basement room. Our flashlights illuminate the former barbershop. It's odd to relate to the Kathy on TV, to know what she doesn't know is coming—the one who has no clue to the impact that night would have on her.

I watch the four-minute segment of the initial questioning a good nine or ten times. Stopping, rewinding and scribbling notes to ensure I have each word written precisely how it was said. Once I finish with the recording portion of the footage, I review my transcript.

Cheryl speaks on the recorder: "On their TV show, they show a brick was thrown at them. Honestly, I don't believe you guys did this."

She pauses.

All is silent.

"But if it did happen, can you let us know who did it? Please, if you guys did it, can you tell me on the recorder that you did it? Or can you move a stone or something?"

Brief pause.

Janice interjects. "Then you can say look what we've done."

All is quiet except for a little rustling of clothing and a couple of footsteps.

Cheryl continues, "Or if you did it, can you throw another brick across the room?"

No one talks. No one stirs.

"No. I'm sorry that is too much to ask...How 'bout if you move a little bit of plaster, something easy, just to show us you are here?"

Janice adds, "But nothing to hurt anybody."

Cheryl coughs, then continues. "We just want to know you exist."

Now it's time to review the EVP segment and where the possible spirit voices occurred during the questioning.

I take a deep breath. Press Play. I lean forward and concentrate.

Cheryl—"Or if you did it, can you throw another brick across the room?"

1st EVP—Male: "No thank you. We've already done that."

I pause the DVD to look over my transcripts. Janice wasn't talking at that point. There was no noise in the room at all. I smile, relieved. The polite gentleman spirit EVP must be genuine.

170

Now to the second EVP. I hit Play.

Cheryl—"How 'bout you move a little bit of plaster, something easy, just to show us you are here."
2nd Voice—Didn't mean to hurt anybody.
Cheryl coughs.

I check my notes. This time, Janice had spoken, but the first two words in the EVP are different. My transcripts showed Janice said, "But nothing to hurt anybody."

Very close. I turn up the audio, watching the little green bars move rightward. I listen to it again. Then to the original recording. The last three words of the EVP are definitely Janice's, although her voice sounds a bit different in the suspect EVP than in the initial recording. The cadence is off, the voice a bit smokier. But what about the portion of the EVP that says "Didn't mean?" It seems to override Janice's voice when she said, "But nothing." Both are three syllables in length. However, the EVP doesn't sound anything like "But nothing." It's decidedly different.

I replay it to see if I missed something. But I haven't.

Spirits use the noise around them to make words, according to EVP experts. That's why one type of digital recorder is the most sought out by ghost hunters; they say its internal noise makes it easier for spirits to turn it into words. Strange concept, I must admit. I don't remember who told me this. Perhaps Janice? Cheryl? Someone from a conference past?

I listen one more time and—while I'm not an expert and certainly do not have Janice's extensive knowledge—I know what I hear and it's two spirits. I'm relieved, but a part of me is sad. I hate to dispute Janice's opinion. I'll always respect Janice's opinion and her quest to ferret out questionable evidence. After all, her critical thinking on the paranormal is one of the qualities that initially drew me to her. But then again, I don't know if Janice ever saw the raw footage. Something she could use to analyze and refresh her memory.

I'll just disagree with her in this one instance.

~25~
Being Still

A few blocks from home, I wind my way up the bumpy ATV road on this crisp October morn. The rabbit brush glows yellow with bountiful blooms. Overly stuffed, motionless white clouds fill the sky. It takes great effort to push my leaden legs up the gentle grade, my head pounding in time with my heart. However, I find joy in that I can take a stroll, as for so many years this ability was just a fading dream. I look out over the valley, the new home sprawl engulfing old pastures. I resume walking, breathing hard while staring at the path ahead of me. I step over a lizard's tail-drag print so I will not disturb this evidence of life.

I find my boulder, the one near the scraggly, lop-sided juniper laden with frosty-blue berries. Oblong and flat, this granite rock is as accommodating as a chair. I gently lower my aching body onto it. My legs are so stiff, they don't easily bend.

Once, I thought meditation a flighty activity taken on by Pollyannas who can visualize world peace, but cannot feel God. Over the years, I heard preachers call this practice un-Christian. I'd never questioned it. I'd believed them. But not any more.

In meditation, I find a calmness where I'm still and wait on the Lord. It is my silent prayer, my commune with the Lord. I dedicate five to ten minutes most days to create an invitation to The Great I Am. One that says, "I'll listen." So I sit in the sun. In the wind. In the fleeting sprinkles that only in Nevada could be called rain.

Traditional prayer still has its place in my recently renovated beliefs. But I find prayer by itself limiting. It's as if I'm talking *at* God: a one-way communication as I go through my laundry lists of requests and thanks. Please help my Dad's knee surgery go well. Thank you for giving me the strength to work 25 hours a week and to do more than the Mayo Clinic said I'd ever be able to. Thank you for letting me experience Goldfield.

I inhale deeply. Once. Twice. Three times. My hands chill as I set my palms atop my thighs and start by praying. For the day's protection. For Ken's protection. And thanks. Then, I ask the Great I Am what I need to know. I quiet my mind and wait, as I've done dozens and dozens of instances over the past months.

At times, I fancy I hear God in the jackrabbit scurrying through the aromatic sagebrush, the wing flaps of a raven overhead or the giddy laughter of a small girl running alongside her puppy. This morning, though, all I hear is the occasional rumble of a semi cruising down the Pyramid Highway and the distant echoes of target shooting.

The sun caresses me, its warm tendrils chase away the morning chill. I welcome it and let its heat penetrate my very core.

Then it happens.

A surge of electricity tingles my fingertips and quickly moves into my hands. Then my arms. To the top of my skull, down into my heart and reaching toward my toes. My whole body vibrates internally, as if each atom's being jump-started. Awakened.

I've only had one instance of spirit contact while meditating. Well over a month ago when Ruby came to visit me just prior to Goldfield. The energy intensifies, pulsates as if my body were one giant heart. "Is someone here?" I say a bit shakily.

"Yes." A male voice resonates inside my head.

I sit up a bit straighter. This is something special, something significant. And I know in my gut, this will be more than just a visit.

"Do I know you?" I whisper aloud.

"No. But I have always been with you." His tone is strong, compassionate.

An overwhelming purity of love mixes with the electrical impulses coursing through my body. *He's always been here.* In a way, I know that. I know this love from somewhere. From my past.

If it were night, I imagine the glow I feel would appear like a thousand incandescent bulbs. The pulses remain strong—if they were any more intense, it'd be painful. "What are you doing? What is this sensation?"

"I'm healing you."

Did I hear him correctly? "You're...you're healing me?" Each cell in my body is being shocked awake. Please let this be true. Please let me not imagine this!

"Yes," the voice says.

I'd stopped asking for healing years ago, when I'd come to realize God doesn't answer our prayers in the ways we expect. And the Great I Am has a purpose for everything. Illness makes over my personality and grows my soul. Experiences shaping the essence of who I am to become. I'm more patient, appreciative and sympathetic to others. Although, I must admit, when I'm at my lowest, I question the importance of lessons coming at the cost of my health, my youth and my ability to bear children.

Love washes over me, embracing me in a divine hug. As if the Lord's arms have reached down from Heaven and swept me into the air. Warm. Radiant. Pure. Intensity beyond anything earthly. Love so intense. Heavenly joy! Tears well in my eyes.

"Thank you! Please, thank God," I exclaim. The energy flowing into me eases into a pleasant prickliness, similar to that of an electronic massage chair. "Why me?" This comes out of my mouth before I realize it. I don't mean to sound ungrateful. But why me, when there are people dying from their afflictions?

"God has a purpose for you. You must be healthy to achieve the goal God has set for you." It occurs to me then this heavenly voice belongs to an angel.

God has a goal for me! God wants me healthy! Tears stream down my cheeks. Their saltiness seeps through my parted lips into my mouth. The electrical impulses push down through my body out through my feet into the sandy earth. The pain, a constant that's dogged me for 18 years, softens, almost liquefying as it drains out of me. My head, limbs lighten—free of the weakness chaining my mass to gravity. Without effort, I raise my face to the sky, my eyes still closed. I'm being healed. Renewed. I now possess a strength I don't believe I've ever felt before.

A nearby quail voices a "Where are you? Where are you?" call. A distant bird hoarsely replies. I sit on this boulder, not sure what to say. What to do. Then I recall Vickie's class. How she said when you make contact, ask for validation. But it seems ungrateful to ask for proof with a blessing of this magnitude.

The pain vanquished. Completely gone! My body lightens. With clarity, I know I'm healed. My body's livened. The love enveloping me unmistakable. I'm drenched in a love reminiscent of when I accepted Christ as my Savior. Decades ago.

Still, I know my logical mind will start to doubt this miracle. So I ask, "Please don't get me wrong. I believe what you are doing. I accept God's glorious gift," I say in a shaky whisper. "But. But, can you show me something that'll happen to me in the next week, so I know this really happened? That this isn't some wonderful dream?"

No answer.

I shouldn't have made this request. I'm insolent. How dare I ask the Great I Am's messenger for further proof, when I've just been raised to the mountaintop! "I'm sorry. I'm so sorry. I shouldn't have asked. Forget what I said. *Please.*"

I quiet myself, hoping for a reply. I keep my mind empty, so the angel can fill it. I wait. For what seems minutes. I'm about to give up meditating when a movie starts to play inside my brain, a film where the camera's perspective is through my own eyes. This has never happened before. I concentrate on the back of my mind. Ken and I enter a crowded room in a restaurant. Two long tables draped in rose-colored cloths. Dark wood covers the walls half way up, Victorian style wallpaper runs up to the dark ceiling. A large, framed mirror hangs on one wall with sconce lighting on either side of it. It's an old room in an old building. A place I've never been before. People are laughing. Then I see De, our friend. There are balloons. It's a party. *Ahh, it's De's party.* Soon, we're to travel to Ashland, Oregon for her surprise gala. That must be it. I try to remember every minute detail.

Then, the movie stops, runs to black.

"Thank you. Thank you so much."

No reply. The love lifts. My angel has gone.

I open my eyes, the morning light momentarily burning the color from my vision. I push myself off the boulder with an incredible ease, almost launching myself across the rutted dirt road. I haven't experienced lightness such as this since my 20s—it's as if lead scales have dropped off every part of my once-dragging body. My legs are strong. My muscles loosen. I want to move. To dance. To sing my praises to God.

I lift my hands to the heavens. "Thank you!" I shout to the high desert landscape. "I will do whatever you want, Lord!" To the junipers. To the quail frozen under the nearby sagebrush. This is a miracle. Miracles do happen. And it happened to me!

I wonder about the Great I Am's goal for me. I should've asked what it was. *No. No, I shouldn't.* God is in control. The Lord has a plan and works wonders. This is a time to rejoice. Not to question, but to celebrate. To acknowledge the Great I Am's awesome power.

I tentatively skip down the dirt road and sing a hymn I've always loved. "I love you Lord…"

My body moves easily, like a red tail hawk soaring the currents. My skipping becomes seamless: knees kick up with each hop just like when I was a kid in a pink polyester mini-dress and white knee socks. I'm laughing. Crying.

Today, I'm blessed to receive further proof that God never leaves me (or anyone else) alone. Societal pressures, which drove me to think like the masses, squelched my instinct to be more receptive to the larger world around me. To open up, connect and truly accept the Lord's here beside me.

Between God's loving scolding a while back and my experience through the angelic messenger today, the Great I Am's presence in my life is as deeply rooted in my brain now as it has always been in my heart. A fact. Not a theory based on faith alone. I've always had faith. Now I have a physical miracle. Like the blind man Jesus gave sight to. With a surety that can only come through experiencing a miracle, my eyes have been given true sight. For this moment, I see. I'll do whatever God wants me to do. This imperfect, sinful person is loved. The Most Supreme of All Beings loves me and finds me worthy of healing!

~26~
Celebration

Although I'm 46, my mind and body have traveled back in time, revitalized. Thinking and focusing take no effort. The disease's cognitive complications vanished along with the physical symptoms. I no longer dread going to bed, as I fall asleep within 30 minutes of lying down, and I sleep a solid seven hours, usually only waking once during the night. My endless sugar cravings have ceased. And my disposition is the "Old Kathy," more carefree and optimistic. My skin, joints and muscles no longer throb with painful inflammation. I can stand for long periods without getting dizzy or having to find a wall to lean against. Life is so good!

The radio plays as I rinse the dishes. The warm water caresses my hands, turning them pink. I arrange the plates in the bottom shelf of the dishwasher. It's funny how great it is to wash dishes after work, instead of laying on the couch, a cranky lump, until it's time for bed.

U2's "Beautiful Day" comes on. I dry my hands and turn up the volume on the tinny, cheap radio. I dance across the kitchen floor, wiggling my hips and waving the dishtowel over my head.

I marvel how easy it is to dance: the freeness with which I swing my hips, wave my arms. How wondrous it feels not to fight my muscles. To not wince in pain from moving this way or that. I slide along the kitchen linoleum and focus on nothing but my body's flow. Finally, I'm free of stiffness. Now, I'm light.

Why did I have to endure almost two decades of brutalizing pain, mental fog and weakness? Perhaps, God waited to heal me until I trusted the Lord enough to relinquish control over my life, and realized I didn't have to be healthy to be happy.

Each day of this illness had consisted of hard-fought battles. Keeping a positive attitude and not permanently giving in to the darkness, a self-pity that would overtake me if I thought of my future or even worse, the past and what I'd missed. Plodding through my physical therapy exercises, which had been more in line with moving granite than stretching muscles. Or laboring on a crossword puzzle to get my brain to build new connections and function more consistently. I did what I could to treat my body, which had betrayed me, with respect, reverence. After all, God had gotten me out of bed, granting me enough strength, energy to work 25 hours a week and take an occasional three-mile hike. And I'd been so thankful for that gift.

I grab the rinsed wooden spoon and pound an air drum to the beat. The front blinds are open; someone could see me prancing around in my revelry, but I don't care.

The Great I Am had blessed me by getting me through my bed-ridden hell and allowing me some quality of life. I'd accepted the gift God granted me ten or so years ago. In gratitude, I stopped praying for complete health.

I'd moved on. If I'd still begged the Lord to heal me, to give me back my life, would I have experienced this miracle? The Almighty's timetable is divinely inspired. Who am I to determine when I would've been ready to accept my restoration?

The song ends. I lower the volume; put the last of the glasses and silverware in the dishwasher. I take a paper towel and clean up the water drops on the counter. Then stroll down the hall to see what Ken is up to.

He's reading his e-mail in the den. I peck him on the cheek as he sits at the computer desk stacked with papers.

He stops and studies me.

I can't quite read what's on his face. But, I'm hoping he's noticed. "What's up?" I ask.

"You. What's gotten into you?" he asks as his eyes scan my face.

I smile so large, I can feel the stretch against my cheeks. *This is it.* "What do you mean?"

"You're acting like you did before you got sick."

I laugh. It's time to tell him. Ken needed to witness my transformation for himself. So he'll better accept it. Ken's never been a church person—his spirituality comes from nature where he feels most at home. I'm curious to see how he'll accept my news.

Ken speaks up. "Are you doing something different? You seem like your old self. What's going on?" He looks almost concerned. "You have all this energy. You're happy. You're walking around the house singing." He swings the office chair around to face me.

I bend over and hug him.

"It's amazing," I say as I stand back up. I've rehearsed this moment. I want it to be meaningful, believable to him. But the static words I practiced didn't feel like they'd give my news its full due.

"What's amazing?"

The butterflies in my stomach beat their wings. Just like my ghost stories, my healing sounds preposterous, out there. But just like my ghost stories, this is true. I clear my throat. God deserves all the glory. "Oh, Ken, it's a miracle!" The words tumble out. "God healed me. I was on my walk a little while back. I was told I have a greater purpose, so I need my health. I feel wonderful."

Ken stares at me.

I take his hand. "When it happened, I felt this burst of electricity run into my fingertips and throughout my body. And the pain, it all went away. I'm sleeping. I can think. My body feels light! I'm healed. It is a miracle!" My eyes tear up, as the emotions of the moment come streaming back to me. The love. The power. The compassion.

Ken hops up from the office chair and bear hugs me. "I've been watching you for a couple of days now, wondering...."

I tighten my arms around him. "I'm so excited. I'm so glad you noticed. I wanted you to see it for yourself. Before I told you. I know it all sounds too weird."

Ken pulls back to look at me, his hands remain on my waist. "That's great....But what else are you doing? Are you taking new medications? Did the therapist try a different treatment on you?"

I look into his eyes, which tonight mirror the blue of his shirt. What a shock this must be to him. "It was God. I haven't done anything different. The Lord healed me. Miracles do happen!"

"Well, that's just wonderful!" His voice chokes up. My news has finally sunk in. "So wonderful."

God wants us to be discerning, yet open. To seek out divine guidance and build a closer relationship with the Most Holy. I read Acts 28:27 with new insight.

> *For this people's heart has become calloused;*
> *They hardly hear with their ears,*
> *And they have closed their eyes.*
> *Otherwise, they might see with their eyes,*
> *Hear with their ears,*
> *Understand with their hearts*
> *And in turn, I would heal them. (NIV)*

Once I mentally accepted I could hear God, angels and spirits communicate with me, I opened up as never before and received healing. We all possess the ability to tap into the spirit realm, so we can better connect with God and divine emissaries. We've been gifted with heavenly tools, such as psychic abilities, to help us on our earthly journeys.

I read 1 Thessalonians 5:19-22.

> *Do not put out the spirit's fire;*
> *Do not treat prophesies with contempt.*
> *Test everything.*
> *Hold on to the good.*
> *Avoid every kind of evil. (NIV)*

I pray every day to be open to divine guidance, to fulfill the purpose the Lord's set forth for me upon this earth.

I've grown so much in the time since Goldfield. For one, *God is real.* The Almighty's not some ethereal being I can't feel, can't hear. The Lord's not stuck up in heaven far removed from me. Rather, God's beside me, urging me to pay attention and not discount experiences that society, logic and some religious institutions discourage.

I'd fought the paranormal incidents in my life, thinking they all came from the dark side. But the evidence—the bountiful harvest of blessings resulting from what started that night in Goldfield—are all too positive to be anything of Satan. As Jesus said, a house divided cannot stand. And the devil would never do anything to help me forge a closer relationship with God.

Yes, I believe evil is in the spirit realm, just as it is on earth. But God has given us discernment, protection if we only ask for them.

At a red light in Medford, Oregon, Ken digs the e-mail with directions to the restaurant's location out of his shirt breast pocket and hands it to me. Last night, the party location was moved from a Mexican restaurant to a place called Porters. We drive through the old downtown, its multi-story brick buildings, small mom and pop stores, railroad tracks.

I'm alert, energetic and happy. Free. I hope there's dancing. I want to move all night.

I almost miss our turn. "Ohh. Up here, turn left at the light." I squirm. *Please let the mind movie be right.* I'm not sure why this is so important to me, as I know my health's restored. I guess the validation of having this vision come true is proof this healing will stick.

Ken looks for oncoming traffic and makes the turn. "There it is." He points to the right.

There's the sign, Porters, alongside an old railroad depot! My heart quickens.

We park the car and I'm out as soon as Ken brakes. "Come on!" I say, barely able to control my excitement.

"Wait," he says as he steps out. "We need to grab De's card."

I open the back door and grab the envelope off the seat.

"Should I get our coats out of the trunk?" Ken asks.

"No." I grab his arm affectionately and guide him to the entrance. I hold my head high and match Ken's long strides with little effort. I can't get to the party soon enough. I clench my hands, my stomach churns with acid. *Please let this be the movie.* The hostess takes us into the restaurant. Railroad antiques hang from the dark wood paneling.

"We're going to have so much fun!" I look at Ken. He places his hand low on my back as we follow the hostess through the dining room. She then turns right through two double French doors. I hear a crowd.

I want to be last in the room. I want Ken to go ahead of me, as I don't know what emotions will play on my face. Ken starts to guide me, when I see an old railroad lantern. "Oooh, Dad would love this, wouldn't he? I just want to give it a quick look." I pull away, glance at it.

Ken's just in front of me as I follow him into the private dining area. The darkly paneled and wallpapered room has a large long mirror, sconces and two long tables with rose-colored tablecloths. Exactly how I saw it in my head! I want to shout, dance and jump up and down all at the same time!

Ken places his arm around my waist. We look at each other and then shout, "Happy Birthday, De!"

She turns to us, wide-eyed, giggling. "Kathy, Ken!"

I laugh while fighting back tears of elation. "Let's party!"

~Acknowledgments~

This amazing journey I've been on was made possible through the generosity of others.

When I first met Janice Oberding, I had no inkling she would become a major player in my spiritual growth. Over the years, Janice has encouraged and empowered me to think expansively, and to open my mind and heart to the unknown. I'll always respect her skepticism, passion and expertise.

Of course, this story wouldn't have taken place if it hadn't been for KTVN Channel 2 in Reno, Nevada. Former reporter/anchor Bill Brown epitomizes generosity and I am forever grateful to him for inviting me to participate. Thank you to Jeff Foss, KTVN's chief videographer, who made me feel welcome from the first moment we met. And to Kevin Bennett, KTVN's former executive producer, who made the feature news series fly. "Cheryl" and "Ted," thank you for all you taught me and your support during my emotional aftermath following Goldfield.

Virginia Ridgway, caretaker of the Goldfield Hotel, cleared our path to staying the night in that wonderful "Gem of the Desert." Thank you for allowing us to experience the energies that inhabit the hotel and for caring about the unseen entities who call the hotel home.

Then, there are my former supervisors at Truckee Meadows Community College who prodded me beyond my comfort level. Kathy Odynski, thank you for insisting I help coordinate the fledgling Nevada Ghost Conference that pushed me to deal with people whom I would've been too judgmental to work with otherwise. And my appreciation goes out to Michael Rainey for encouraging me to venture to Goldfield as part of my job as the division's publicist.

Through the Nevada Ghost and Paranormal Series, I've met an amazingly diverse population of people—psychics, scientists, believers, skeptics and religious leaders. Every instructor has helped me in some way, whether they embraced the paranormal or not. I thank you all for allowing me to learn why you believe as you do. I especially want to thank medium Vickie Gay for her friendship, support and advice.

To "Charlotte" who took a chance by revealing her amazing God-given gifts and offering ongoing support over all these years, you never let me down or let me struggle too long with the unknown. I respect that you expected me to work out elements of my experience on my own, while insisting you'd always be there when I needed it.

Writing is a solitary endeavor, but strong writing results from great, constructive feedback. I'm indebted to the illustrious women who made up our regular writing critique group—Doresa Banning (editor extraordinaire), Marti Benjamin, Barbara Hunt and Pat Holland Conner—for all the hours you spent reviewing my manuscript and blog posts. Doresa, you are a brilliant editor and I've been blessed to work with you. Barbara, thank you for giving your time and excellent proofing eye to polishing up my book's final draft. The four of us started as strangers, but now we're great friends. Thank you for being my cheerleaders when I wanted to give up. I also appreciate Erin Granat's gentle prodding for me to enroll into a memoir writing class, even though I swore I would never write about Goldfield. In addition, I appreciate those authors who read and provided suggestions on my manuscript: Victoria Ford and Linda Talbot. Thank you as well to Tom and Lisa Butler, directors of the Association of TransCommunication, for reading my manuscript and writing an advance testimonial for this book.

To build an author's platform nowadays takes the assistance of experts in their fields. Cal Anderson, a well-rounded technology guru, designed and maintained my wonderful website. Paula Napo created the striking artwork for my website and designed my book cover. Amy Ellis made me look good in promotional videos. You three are angels on earth for freely giving so much of your time and talent to help me succeed.

Ken Johns, your love has held me up during the very worst of times. You stayed by my side through years of debilitating illness. You encouraged me to pursue my literary dream, even if it meant me spending countless weekends at the computer. Thank you for believing in me, even though I know you still have difficulty believing in the paranormal. When my life has taken surprising turns, you've always remained beside me and for that, I'm eternally grateful.

All that I've accomplished in life is thanks to the foundation my parents Bryan and Darlene created for me. Having a loving, supportive childhood where I came to believe I could do anything is still a gift I hold very precious. Thank you for the happy, well-adjusted childhood you provided me and for never losing faith in me.

And, to the Great I Am for demonstrating your boundless and patient love, I will do anything to serve you.

~About the Author~

Kathleen Berry. Photo by Ken M. Johns.

Kathleen's worked with ghost hunters, psychics, mediums and scientists since the community college that she works for started offering noncredit paranormal programs in 2002. Although her job responsibilities are comprised primarily of marketing noncredit programs, she became the manager of the Nevada Ghost and Paranormal Series in 2008 and has coordinated it ever since.

Once a freelance writer, Kathleen has sold dozens of articles to publications ranging from international periodicals and in-flight magazines to an array of regional publications. She also manages the TMCC Writers' Conference, held each April in Reno, Nevada.

During her free time, she enjoys kayaking and hiking the wilds of the American West with her significant other, Ken.

16128877R00115

Made in the USA
San Bernardino, CA
20 October 2014